Identity Theft

Uncovering the Truth about
Black History in the Bible

by

Keenan West

Watersprings
PUBLISHING

Published by Watersprings Publishing, a division of
Watersprings Media House, LLC.
P.O. BOX 1284
Olive Branch, MS 38654
www.waterspringsmedia.com
Contact publisher for bulk orders and permission requests.

Copyrights © 2020 by Keenan West

All rights reserved. No part of this publication may be reproduced, distributed, or transmitted in any form or by any means, including photocopying, recording, or other electronic or mechanical methods, without the prior written permission of the publisher, except in the case of brief quotations embodied in critical reviews and certain other noncommercial uses permitted by copyright law.

Printed in the United States of America.

Library of Congress Control Number: 2020919871

ISBN-13: 978-1-948877-70-1

Table of Contents

	Preface	1
	Introduction	3
Chapter 1	In The Beginning	7
Chapter 2	The Father of Black People	16
Chapter 3	I Didn't Know They Were Black	24
Chapter 4	The Real Gentiles	35
Chapter 5	The Black Man's Book	43
Chapter 6	Identity Theft	48
Chapter 7	Black People and the Sabbath	77
Chapter 8	Who Cares?	81
	References	83
	About The Author	84

Preface

How would you feel if you found out that a lot of what you've been taught, with regard to Scripture, has been a lie? How would you feel if you found out that not only were you deceived, but millions if not billions of people around the world have been told the same lies? Would it cause you to change your perspective on scripture? Would it cause you to start to question everything else you have been taught to believe? Would you keep this newfound information to yourself?

These are some of the questions I have grappled with as I have studied and learned that much of what we've been led to believe about the key tenets of scripture are not true. I have also wrestled with the overwhelming burden of whether to share this information or keep it to myself.

This book is a result of the Holy Spirit's confirmation that others need to know the truth. For that reason, I cannot keep silent.

To be clear, I make no claims of being a biblical scholar, theologian, archaeologist, or any other authority on scripture. What I am is a sinner saved by grace who understands that the Bible speaks for itself. The problem is, that for years, we have allowed everyone else to speak for it.

Over the next several pages, it is my desire to inspire others to also allow the Bible to speak for itself and to not merely accept mainstream society's interpretation of it.

I would also like to be clear that the purpose of this book is to in no way denigrate, demean, or condemn any other people group. It is only a presentation of biblical and historical truth.

Introduction

When we look at the state of the black church, one of the things we quickly realize is that there is a growing number of people of color who, if they haven't already left, are on their way out. And while it is safe to acknowledge that there are various reasons for this exodus, what we do know is that more and more of them are leaving because they no longer believe that Christianity is inclusive of people of color.

In fact, there are some religions, such as the Nation of Islam, that promote the belief that Christianity is a white man's religion. They believe that the only reason black people are Christians is because Christianity was a way of keeping our ancestors in bondage when they first arrived in this country as slaves.

However, since this belief is contrary to what the Bible teaches, I believe that it is imperative that we, as African Americans, understand that not only is Christianity not the white man's religion but is very much a religion that has people of color at its roots.

Therefore, it is important for us to read the Bible for ourselves so that we might have a better understanding of how the contents within its pages apply to us.

It was once said, "History is always written by the victors. When two cultures clash, the loser is obliterated, and the winner writes the history books- books which glorify their own cause and disparage the conquered foe (Anonymous)."

For years we have allowed others to write our history. As a result, we have received an inaccurate account of that history.

This is one of the reasons why we are leaving the church and joining many of the "pro-black" conscious and religious groups- because we don't understand the contributions people of color have made, not just to history, but also to the Bible and the development of the Christian faith.

For many of us, we have accepted the lie that Christians worship a white God and that Christianity is a "white man's religion." We have accepted the false narrative that the Bible, and Christianity, were given to our ancestors after they came to this country, in order to keep them in bondage.

But this is not true. Not only does the Bible tell a different story, but history does as well. That is what this book will attempt to uncover.

What must be understood is, that in order to change the consciousness of people of color, you have to begin by changing the information given to the minds of people of color. If that is not changed, the consciousness stays the same. If the consciousness stays the same, we will continue to believe that we are inferior. We will continue to believe that we are 3/5 of a man, that we are nothing but thugs, or any other derogatory belief that mainstream society is trying to portray us as. We will continue to accept the false narrative that we are cursed, and that our lot has always been that we are nothing more than the descendants of slaves.

For that consciousness to change, we need to know that we are more than the picture society has painted of us for the last 400 years. We need to know that "I am somebody," and our people have accomplished more than what the world wants to give us credit for.

Although no one likes to admit it, people of color are responsible for many well-known inventions. For instance, the pyramids, paper, math, pulleys, engineering, food preservation, the pipe organ, embalming, the three-light traffic light, the ironing board, the home security system, and the gas mask- to name a few- were all invented by people of color.

Yet, this is not the history that is taught in our schools. The history we see over and over again is always from a European perspective. We are not made aware of the numerous contributions made by black people. In my opinion, the reason these accomplishments remain hidden is because of the collective effort to keep people of color in slavery. Whether it be physical slavery or mental slavery, we must acknowledge the concerted effort to make sure black people don't know who they are or what they have done.

To combat this effort, I believe it is highly important that we, as black people, educate ourselves. By educating ourselves, it gives us the ability to discern for ourselves what we believe is true and what is not.

Unfortunately, for 400 years, we have not had the privilege of seeing the other side of the story. We have only been given the view that is beneficial to the "victors," those who want to continue to keep us in darkness. When we have a chance to uncover all the facts, we have the opportunity not only to choose what we want to believe but also to choose what we want to do with the information we have now received.

When I think about the overwhelming amount of challenges we face as African-Americans, I can't help but think that it's almost impossible for us to address many of these issues when we really do not understand who we are, where we came from, or how we got to where we are in the first place.

What makes it difficult is that we are probably the only race that is uninformed about who we are as a people. Granted, we know that we came from Africa. We also know we are descendants of slaves, but for the most part, that's pretty much all we know.

For those who have not researched their heritage on any of the numerous DNA or ancestry websites, they have no idea what part of Africa they are from. We have no clue as to the tribe our ancestors belonged. We know nothing of the language they spoke.

While every other race can say that their relatives are from Germany, or Ireland, or wherever, African-Americans do not have that privilege. Since our ancestors were taken as slaves, we are not fortunate enough to have records that show that our great-great-great-great grandfather was a part of the Ashanti tribe in Ghana, or the Igbo tribe in Nigeria, or the Zulu tribe in South Africa. We have very little to prove who we are as a people.

As a result, we don't know who we are. We cannot look back and pinpoint the specific country or tribe in which our ancestors originated. All we know is that over 400 years ago, we were loaded onto boats as slaves. We were then dropped off in the Caribbean, North America, and South America. Over time we would eventually lose our identity.

This is in contrast to the European-Americans who have made sure that "the content of their consciousness was well informed about their greatness. The great stories of Louis XIV, Columbus, Napoleon, Queen Victoria, Copernicus, Galileo, the Greeks, and the Romans are fundamental elements of the informational system that we are given about European-American people. This barrage of information about European and American greatness is systematically given to themselves to ensure that they maintain their consciousness of who they are (Akbar 1996)."

Most African Americans don't have that luxury, they have no clue of their culture, and heritage.

But what would happen if, as African-Americans, we actually knew the truth about who we really are? What would happen if we knew where we came from? What would happen if we understood how important our ancestors were, not just to the foundation of this country, but also to the establishment of Christianity? I wonder how we would carry ourselves differently if we understood that we do not have to fantasize or be proud of a fictional place called Wakanda because we are descendants of real people, and from real places spoken about in scripture.

Some will say, "Why does race matter? Isn't it interesting that only when people try to argue that Jesus, Abraham, or the Hebrews were black the same question, 'Why does race or skin color matter?' comes up. I guess everything is all good if the bible remains white (Dalton Jr. 2014)."

"A poll revealed that the majority of high school biology teachers in America believe that certain races are inherently inferior to others, and Newsweek reported that many Chinese 'adhere to racial hierarchy in which the darker a person's skin color, the lower his status and worth.' These beliefs clearly indicate that biblical teaching regarding racial origins, geographic roots, ethnic heritage, equality before God, and oneness in Christ is desperately needed (McKissic 1990)."

What is interesting is that, because our views have been formed by what we were taught growing up, it's hard for us to see the importance or relevance of anything outside of that.

CHAPTER 1

In The Beginning

Before we can understand who we are today, we first have to understand where we came from and how we got here in the first place. Marcus Garvey once said, "A people without the knowledge of their past history, origin, and culture is like a tree without roots." To begin this journey, we have to start by first discovering our roots. When we can identify the roots and how we came to be, we can be better informed of what our destiny should look like.

When we listen to the abridged version of history that is often taught in our schools, for some reason, the history of African-Americans always begins in 1619. This is insulting because it gives the impression that people of color did not exist before slavery. The reality is that our history began long before our ancestors stepped off of slave ships. That may not be what those in power want us to know, but according to the Bible, our history began in the book of Genesis in a place called the Garden of Eden.

Now, usually, when we think of the Garden of Eden, we don't typically associate it with the continent of Africa. The reason we don't associate it with Africa is because we typically look to Europeans as our source for information. That's somewhat understandable because they write the majority of the historical reference books. They control the media. Therefore, whenever we look for, or are given information about ourselves, we look to sources that don't necessarily have our best interests at heart. That's why the Garden of Eden is not typically associated with Africa. Yet, when we look at scripture, it is clear that the Garden was on the continent of Africa.

Genesis 2:8-14 says,

> *"The Lord God planted a garden eastward in Eden, and there He put the man whom He had formed. And out of the ground the Lord God made every tree grow that is pleasant to the sight and good for food. The tree of life was also in the midst of the garden, and the tree of the knowledge of good and evil.*
>
> *Now a river went out of Eden to water the garden, and from there it parted and became four riverheads. The name of the first is Pishon; it is the one which skirts the whole land of Havilah, where there is gold. And the gold of that land is good. Bdellium and the onyx stone are there. The name of the second river is Gihon; it is the one which goes around the whole land of Cush. The name of the third river is Hiddekel; it is the one which goes toward the east of Assyria. The fourth river is the Euphrates."*

According to verse 8, God planted the garden eastward in Eden. That means that Eden was not just the garden but an actual place. The garden happened to be a place in Eden. It's as if someone told you that they went to the McDonald's in Tennessee. McDonald's is the place, and it is located in the area called Tennessee. In the same way, the garden was located eastward in the place called Eden.

We then have to ask the questions, "Where exactly was Eden? Was it in Europe? Was it in the Middle East? Where exactly was the birthplace of humanity?" These are such important questions because the answers will give us the foundation for where we want to go in the rest of this book.

The blessing is that we don't have to guess where the Garden of Eden was because the Bible gives us its exact location. I don't know about you, but that helps to remove all the guesswork. It also allows us to learn the garden's exact location without having to be influenced by any other sources that may be biased in their conclusions.

In Genesis 2:10, the Bible says,

> *"Now a river went out of Eden to water the garden, and from there it parted and became four riverheads."*

Image via: ("The Garden of Eden," Accessed on Sept.1, 2020, http://www.blackhistoryinthebible.com/africa-and-arabia/the-garden-of-eden/)

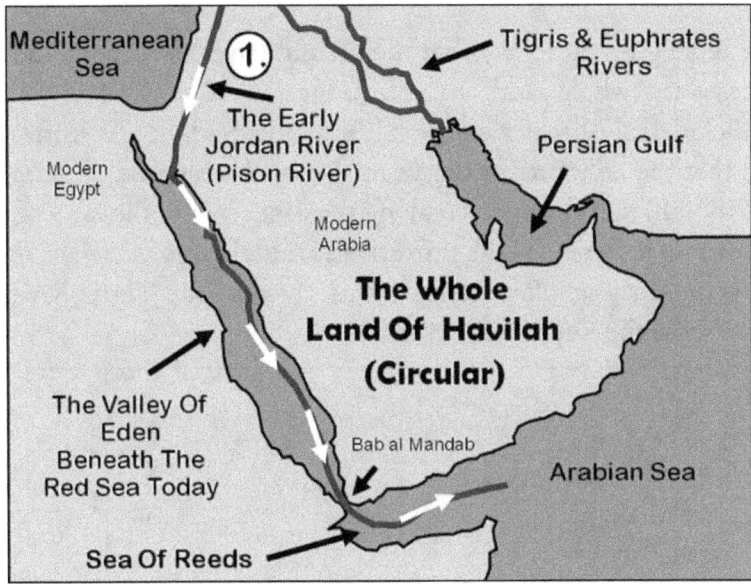

Wherever the Garden of Eden was, there was a river that went out of it and branched off into four different rivers. So, this was not one long river. It also was not four different rivers. According to the text, it was one river that became four different rivers going four different directions.

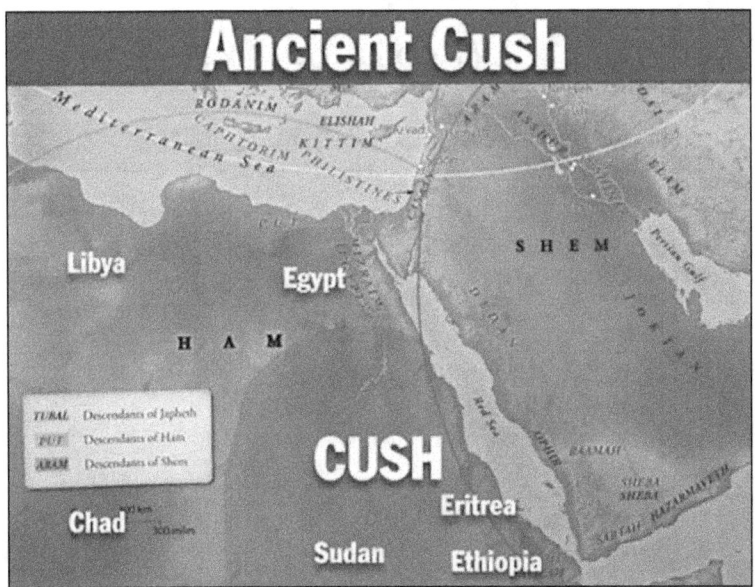

The land of Havilah was the area that we commonly call the "Middle East." The Pishon River is the river that skirts or encompasses this entire area.

The Bible goes on to say that the second (river) is Gihon, and it encompasses the whole land of Cush (Genesis 2:13, NKJV). The land of Cush included the areas we now call Ethiopia, Sudan, and Eritrea. This means that the Gihon river began in the northwest area of the Middle East (Havilah) and came down along the east coast of the land of Cush.

According to verse 14, the third river, Hiddekel, goes toward the east of Assyria. Most scholars identify this river as the Tigris River. The fourth river is the Euphrates River.

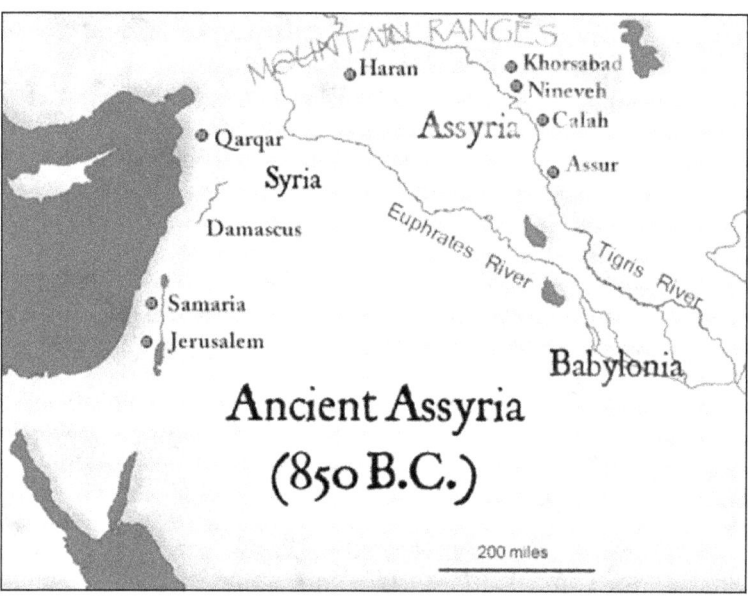

Image via: ("The Lost Rivers of the Garden of Eden - Found," Accessed Sept.1, 2020, https://www.kjvbible.org/rivers_of_the_garden_of_eden.html)

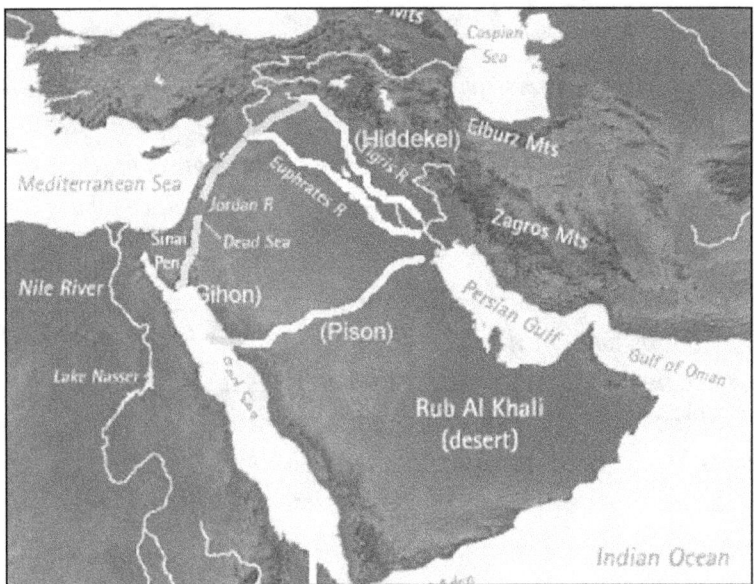

When we look at the map above, we see all four rivers, with the river head being in the northwest area of the "Middle East." That area was initially known as the land of Canaan. Canaan, of course, was the Promised Land that God would eventually lead the children of Israel to. Today that area is called Lebanon. It is believed that the Garden of Eden was most likely in this area called Lebanon. The Bible also gives a clear indication that this assumption is correct.

In Ezekiel 31, Ezekiel compares Assyria to a cedar. At the height of her power, Assyria dominated the Middle East. Assyria's dominance would tower like a cedar higher than all the trees of the field. There were several cities of Assyria that were situated at or near the Tigris River. This strategic location would help to provide much-needed water for these cities. As a result, Assyria would grow like a cedar because of the nourishment it received from the waters. This cedar would be located in Lebanon.

Ezekial 31:3-9 says:

> Indeed Assyria was a cedar in Lebanon,
> With fine branches that shaded the forest, And of high stature;
> And its top was among the thick boughs. The waters made it grow;
> with their RIVERS RUNNING AROUND the place where it was
> planted, And sent out rivulets to all the trees of the field.
>
> Therefore its height was exalted above all the trees of the field; Its
> boughs were multiplied, And its branches became long
> because of the abundance of water, As it sent them out.
> All the birds of the heavens made their nests in its boughs;
> Under its branches all the beasts of the field brought forth their young,
> And in its shadow all great nations made their home.
>
> Thus it was beautiful in its greatness and in the length of its
> branches, Because its roots reached to abundant waters.
> The cedars in the GARDEN OF GOD could not hide it;
> The fir trees were not like its boughs, And the chestnut trees were not
> like its branches; No tree in the GARDEN OF GOD was like it in
> beauty. I made it beautiful with a multitude of branches, So that all the
> trees of EDEN envied it, that were in the GARDEN OF GOD.

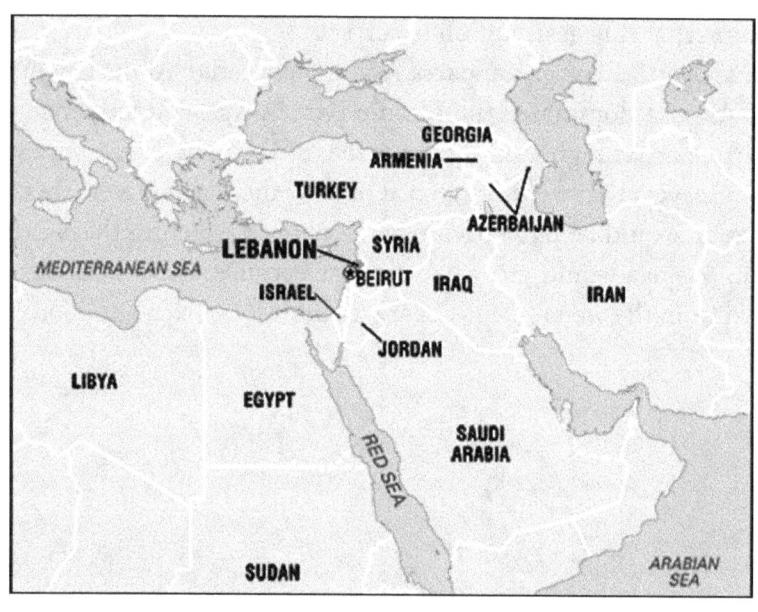

What's interesting is that, if the Garden of Eden was in Lebanon, and the Land of Canaan was also in the area we call Lebanon, then when God sent the children of Israel to the Promised Land, He was actually sending them back (figuratively) to the Garden of Eden. That makes a lot of sense since God never wanted His people to leave the Garden.

One of the things most people are unaware of is the fact that the Middle East was not always called the Middle East. At one time, the "Middle East" was actually considered North Africa. The term Middle East did not come into existence until the 1850s.

It originated in the British India Office as a way to describe the Orient (a term used to describe the East) after it was split into three distinct areas- the Near East, the Middle East, and the Far East. The term was not popularized until 1902 by a man named Alfred Thayer Mahan. Mahan was an American naval strategist who used the name to refer to the region between Arabia and India.

What seems like more than a coincidence is that around the same time North Africa was given the name the Middle East, Ferdinand de Lesseps, the former French consul to Cairo, secured an agreement with the Ottoman governor of Egypt to build a canal 100 miles across the Isthmus of Suez. This canal would be called the Suez Canal. The purpose of the construction of the canal was to connect the Mediterranean Sea to the Red Sea.

When you look at a map of the Middle East, you notice that the Suez Canal goes right through Egypt. It goes right through Egypt because, at one time, it was all one landmass.

As a matter of fact, the Sinai Peninsula, Palestine, and Israel all share the same tectonic plate. That means the area we call Israel (Lebanon) is literally a part of northeast Africa. So, Israel (Lebanon) is actually connected to Egypt because of the Sinai Peninsula.

That begs the question, "If you were trying to disconnect, or disassociate the birthplace of humanity from Africa, wouldn't it be a good idea to build a canal right through Egypt, and rename the piece of land that is no longer connected to Africa something else other than Africa?

If you think about it, it makes a lot of sense. If you want the original inhabitants of that land to forget who they are or who they were, would it not be a good idea to separate them from everything they have ever known and give them a new name?

Have you ever wondered why Europeans always rename the lands they colonize, or why they change the language of the native people? No matter what land they colonize, they always rename the area and change the language of the people.

By renaming the land and changing the language, they erase the native people's history and culture. That's why there are Africans in Senegal and Cameroon who speak French. That's also why there are Africans in Namibia who speak German. By changing the language, and the culture, over time, the people will slowly forget who they are. When they forget who they are, they don't know who God originally intended for them to be. When they don't know who God intended them to be, they don't know what they are able to accomplish.

That's exactly what King Nebuchadnezzar did to the Israelites in Daniel 1. When the Israelites were taken from Jerusalem, Nebuchadnezzar changed their names, their diet, and attempted to change their God. He did this because he wanted them to forget who they were. If he could get them to forget who they were, they wouldn't know where they were from, or what their God originally intended for them to be. This is exactly what the enemy has done to us as a people. Since we don't know who we are, we have no idea what we are capable of. As a result, we are willing to accept whatever label is placed upon us.

In 1915, Alfred Wegener, the chief proponent of Continental Drift, coined the term Pangea. Pangea is the belief/concept that all the landmasses on earth, or all the continents, were at one time connected and formed one giant super-continent. It is believed that through a phenomenon called continental drift, this super-continent separated, and all the continents drifted to where they are today.

Scientists believe this took place over hundreds of millions of years, but creationists believe it happened during or sometime after the flood.

That would make sense because it explains how the animals and the rest of humanity got to the other continents. Since we know they didn't put all the animals on boats and take them to each continent, there has to be some other explanation as to how the animals got there. The only logical conclusion would be that, at one time, every animal was on one landmass before being separated by continental drift.

Could it be possible that the Bible actually gives hints of a time when the earth was one large piece of land? Maybe. In Genesis 10:25 it says, "To Eber were born two sons: the name of one was Peleg, for in his days the earth was divided…" When exactly was the earth divided? Could this mean that, in the days of Peleg, the earth was divided, and before then, there existed one large landmass? We don't know. What we do know is that, at one time, the Middle East was considered North Africa because it was physically a part of Africa. That we know for sure. We also know that at the same time North Africa was renamed, a canal was built that physically separated that piece of land from North Africa.

But why is it so important to disassociate Africa with the Middle East? Isn't that just a part of history? It would be if that piece of land called the Middle East were not home to a place called Israel. Since it is home to Israel, by disassociating Africa with the "Middle East," you automatically remove the African connection to Israel. When you remove the African connection to Israel, you remove any thought that the original inhabitants of Israel were people of African descent.

When we realize that the Middle East was always a part of Africa, and that the term Middle East is not the true geographical name, it becomes easier to determine who were the original occupants of the land of Israel.

If life began in the Garden of Eden and the Garden of Eden was in Africa, and Africa is made up of people of color, then it is safe to assume that society's representation of our first parents as having blue eyes and blond hair is categorically false. It is impossible for every biblical character in every story to be of European descent if most of the stories we read about in scripture took place in a land that was predominantly populated by people of color. It just doesn't make sense. There has to be some other explanation as to why society's representation of the progenitors of the human race are always portrayed as being of European descent. The question is, "Is there another explanation?"

CHAPTER 2

The Father of Black People

*Scripture, science, and secular history attest to the fact
that dark-skinned people were politically, culturally,
and numerically dominant in the ancient world and were the
fathers of civilized society as we know it today (McKissic Sr. 1990).*

I can imagine that's a pretty hard pill to swallow for many. As a matter of fact, I'm sure there are many who, because of their unfamiliarity with history, read a statement like that and consider it to be a little far-fetched. The reason it may sound a little far-fetched, even among many people of color, is because we've been conditioned to believe that everything worth anything had its origin with someone white.

For example, many assume that the touch-tone telephone, caller ID, and fiber-optic cable were all created by someone of European descent when they were all invented by a black woman name Dr. Shirley Jackson. So, our assumptions don't line up with the facts.

This is similar to how we have been conditioned to believe that the progenitors of the human race were of European descent, yet when you look at the scriptural evidence, it becomes abundantly clear that there's more truth to the fact that dark-skinned people were politically, culturally and numerically dominant than many would like to admit.

As we learned in chapter one, according to Genesis 2, life as we know it began in North Africa, which is the area we today call the Middle East.

By the time we get to chapter 6, man has gotten so evil that God sends a flood to destroy every living thing on the planet. "But Noah found grace in the eyes of the Lord," God spared him and his family (Genesis 6:8, NKJV).

When we get to chapter 9, the water has receded, and Noah's sons are given the task of repopulating the earth. Noah's three sons were Shem, Ham, and Japheth.

Genesis 9:18-19 says,

"Now the sons of Noah who went out of the ark were Shem, Ham, and Japheth. And Ham was the father of Canaan. These three were the sons of Noah, and from these the whole earth was populated."

According to the text, everybody on the earth is a descendant of one of Noah's three sons- Shem, Ham, and Japheth. Shem would be the progenitor of the Hebrews. Ham would be the father of black people. Japheth would be the ancestor of white people. Every other "race" would find their ancestry through one of these three sons.

Before we prove how this is true, let's first address the elephant in the room.

Noah's Curse

Immediately after the Bible mentions that Noah's three sons would repopulate the earth, we find the account of the events that led to Ham's youngest son being cursed by Ham's father, Noah. It's important to address this story because many lies have been told because of intentional, or unintentional misinterpretations of this story.

According to the story, Ham finds his father drunk and uncovered in his tent. When he sees his father's condition, he goes and tells his brothers that their father is inside the tent naked and inebriated. Shem and Japheth then take a garment and walk backward into the tent and cover up their father. When Noah awakes, he curses his grandson, Canaan. It doesn't say he cursed Ham. It says he cursed Canaan. This is clear from scripture. Yet, over time, certain religious groups proclaimed a version of this story that states that the curse was placed on Ham. Since Ham is the father of all black people, there are many people who teach that all black people are cursed.

Unfortunately, there are several fallacies associated with this interpretation.

First of all, the Bible clearly states that it was Canaan that was cursed and not Ham. In Genesis 9:24-25 it says that Noah "...awoke from his wine, and knew what his younger son had done to him."

"In Hebrew Scripture there is no word for grandson, so when Noah cursed his 'younger son' it was actually a curse on his grandson Canaan, since Hebrew Scriptures do not separate generations into grandsons and great-grandsons and so forth. In those days, they referred to a grandson or great-grandson simply as 'son' much like the Jewish woman that Jesus called a 'daughter of Abraham' when 'father Abraham' had no daughters of record. Recall the Jews called Abraham their father and not their great, great, great, etc, great grandfather (Warden Jr. 2015)."

Another example of this term being used is when Christ is called the "son of David," even though He was not David's son. Christ was Joseph's son. Christ would come onto the scene thousands of years after David died. Therefore, it's impossible for Him to be David's son.

This is why verse 25 clearly states that Canaan was cursed, and not Ham. Yet, despite the clear evidence in Scripture, this false teaching has been taught for decades.

> *"Ham has been so maligned by European theologians*
> *as cursed that institutions that train men and women*
> *to be pastors, ministers, counselors, and priests such as*
> *Bible colleges and seminaries have incorporated his name into the*
> *theological course that studies the curse of sin (Warden Jr. 2015)."*

This takes place despite the fact that scripture is clear, that not only was Ham not cursed, but Noah didn't even feel as though Ham did anything wrong. If he did, he would have mentioned Ham in the curse. Since he doesn't mention Ham in the curse, we would have to assume that he didn't have a problem with what Ham did.

The question we have to ask is, "Why was Canaan cursed?" What did he do that was so bad that it caused his grandfather to curse him? If you think about it, it had to be ill-behaved because not only does Noah curse him, but he curses Canaan's descendants and says that Canaan will be a servant to his two brothers. So, whatever it was, it had to be bad.

In verse 21, it says that Noah got drunk and "became uncovered" under his tent. It is important to notice that it does not say that Noah uncovered himself. The text says, "he became uncovered." That means it is possible that somebody may have uncovered him. When we think of being uncovered, we probably think of it as being mischievous, but not necessarily warranting being cursed. Unfortunately, scripture has a

more sinister definition for when someone uncovers another.
Leviticus 20:11 says,

> "The man who lies with his father's wife has uncovered his father's nakedness; both of them shall surely be put to death. Their blood shall be upon them."

In verse 17, it says,

> "If a man takes his sister, his father's daughter or his mother's daughter, and sees her nakedness and she sees his nakedness, it is a wicked thing. And they shall be cut off in the sight of their people. He has uncovered his sister's nakedness. He shall bear his guilt."

In verse 19, it says,

> "You shall not uncover the nakedness of your mother's sister nor of your father's sister, for that would uncover his near of kin. They shall bear their guilt."

In verse 20, it says,

> "If a man lies with his uncle's wife, he has uncovered his uncle's nakedness. They shall bear their sin; they shall die childless."

When we look at these four texts, in reference to "uncovering one's nakedness," Leviticus gives the impression that the act can denote being intimate with someone (v.20, NKJV), seeing a person naked (v.17, NKJV), or physically uncovering them (v.19, NKJV).

Although there is no clear definition as to exactly what Canaan did when he uncovered his grandfather, what we do know is that it was Canaan who was responsible for the act and not Ham. We also know that whatever Canaan did, it was so bad that, not only does Noah curse Canaan, but he also cursed Canaan's descendants as well.

I'm sure this is hard for many of us because we may have never heard of Canaan being cursed due to him being intimate with his grandfather, even though that is what the scripture defines as "uncovering one's nakedness."

What is interesting is that in Genesis 9:24, it says, "So Noah awoke from his wine, and knew what his younger son had done to him." This is interesting because it would lead you to believe that Noah already knew something about his grandson that isn't explicitly expressed in the text.

It reminds me of that one family member we all seem to have, who because they're known for stealing, they're the first one you look for when something comes up missing at the family reunion.

I can imagine that may have been the case with Canaan. Since Noah knew what kind of person his grandson was, when he woke up to find himself uncovered, the first person he thought about was Canaan.

That explanation seems to be a lot more plausible than the false teaching that, even to this day, continues to be taught in schools and pulpits around the country that Ham and his descendants are cursed.

Ham

Many scholars believe that Ham was the father of black people. This is such a widespread belief that it's not something that's necessarily doubted or questioned in many theological circles. The reason is because the evidence strongly points to no other conclusion.

In Hebrew, the name 'Ham' means hot. According to the Easton's Bible Dictionary, it says that Ham is also an Egyptian word meaning "black." In scripture, Ham is often referred to as Egypt (Psalms 105:23, 26-27; 106:21-22, NKVJ). In Merriam-Webster's Dictionary, Ham is said to be the progenitor of the Egyptians, Nubians, and Canaanites. Even when you look at most maps that depict the Table of Nations, Ham is always designated in the area that today represents Africa.

According to scripture, Ham would have four sons named Cush, Mizraim, Put, and Canaan (Genesis10:6, NKJV). Cush would be the founder of the area known today as Ethiopia, Sudan, and Eritrea. The word "Cush" also means black. Cush would be the father of the Cushites.

Even though today, that area is called Ethiopia (Cush and Ethiopia are used interchangeably in Scripture), that was not its original name. The name Ethiopia was purported to have been given by the Europeans because it means "The land (country) of burnt faces." The Greek word for burned is "ethios," and the word for face was "ops." Therefore "ethios" plus "ops" became Ethiopia. Ethiopia is also one of the first countries mentioned in scripture, first appearing in Genesis 2:13, NKJV.

That one fact alone should tell us everything we need to know about what the original people of that area looked like. According to the Europeans who named the area, the people living their had burnt faces. It's important to note that they were not light-skinned, or olive complexioned, as many like to suggest.

The original people in the land of Cush were people with "burnt faces" or black people. The only reason you find people with lighter complexions there today is because of the Muslim conquests in the seventh century.

According to Britannica.com, there was an Arab invasion in North Africa between 639-642. The invasion was led by the prominent Muslim general Amr Ibn al-Aas. During this time, North Africa would lose its heritage and embrace a new language, a new religion, and a new culture. When this happened, the people began to become lighter due to the influx of Arab people. Before then, the people living there were black.

In fact, "Most Arabs today are descendants of Northern Turkish people and Europeans. There have been studies that prove that the DNA of most Arabs is over 60% Northern Turkish/European vs. 20% African. This is the reason why many Arabs look European with white skin and often different color eyes similar to European Caucasians (Dalton Jr. 2014)."

Another reason why many of the people in that area today have lighter complexions is because of the mixing of Arabs and Europeans over the centuries. Before that, the people of Cush/Ethiopians were black.

Ham's second son, Mizraim, was the founder of the area we call Egypt. And just like Ethiopia, Egypt was not always called Egypt. Like Ethiopia, Egypt was the name given to that particular area by the Greeks. That area was originally called Kemet. Kemet means "land of the black people." Does anybody see a pattern here? I know I do.

Ham has Cush, who founded Ethiopia. He has Mizraim, who was the founder of Egypt. He also has Put (Phut), who would found the area we today call Libya. His last child would be Canaan.

Canaan would found the area we call Palestine, Israel, Lebanon, the western parts of Jordan, and Syria.

What's interesting about Canaan is that the Land of Canaan was also considered the Promised Land. When you look at a map of where the Garden of Eden was, you also notice that the Garden was in the same area that was referred to as the Land of Canaan. That means, after God kicked Adam and Eve out of the Garden, he sent the children of Israel back to the Garden (Canaan) after they left slavery.

I think this makes a whole lot of sense, seeing that God never intended for Adam and Eve to leave the Garden. So, Him designating Canaan as the Promised Land sounds like He wanted to send His people back to their original birthplace.

Another interesting note about Canaan is that, because we know Canaan's father Ham was black, that also means Canaan was black. If Canaan was black, the inhabitants of Canaan (Canaanites) had to have also been black since they were descendants of Canaan.

As a matter of fact, look at what it says in Genesis 10:15-20:

"Canaan begot Sidon his firstborn, and Heth; the Jebusite, the Amorite, and the Girgashite; the Hivite, the Arkite, and the Sinite; the Arvadite, the Zemarite, and the Hamathite. Afterward the families of the Canaanites were dispersed. And the border of the Canaanites was from Sidon as you go toward Gerar, as far as Gaza; then as you go toward Sodom, Gomorrah, Admah, and Zeboiim, as far as Lasha. These were the sons of Ham, according to their families, according to their languages, in their lands and in their nations."

All of these groups, the Jebusites, the Amorites, the Sinites, etc., were all considered Canaanites because they were descendants of Canaan. They were also all black. So the land that would eventually become the Promised Land was full of black people.

I don't know about you, but when I hear people talk about the Canaanites, I never hear them mention the Canaanites being black. Could it be that, if we acknowledge that the Canaanites were black, we would then have to acknowledge that there were other groups in that area that were also black? If there were other groups in that area that were black, could that also mean that much of the historical accounts that we've been given about the inhabitants of that land are also inaccurate?

In Genesis 10:6, it mentions that Ham had four sons, Cush, Mizraim, Put, and Canaan. In verses 15-20, it gives us the lineage of Canaan. In verses 13-14, we find the lineage of Mizraim.

In verse 13, it says,

"Mizraim begot Ludim, Anamim, Lehabim, Naphtuhim, Pathrusim, and Casluhim (from whom came the Philistines and Caphtorim)."

According to the text, the Philistines came from Pathrusim and Casluhim. Pathrusim and Casluhim were descendants of Mizraim. Mizraim would have been black since his father Ham was black. That means the Philistines we read about throughout the Old Testament were also black.

What if I told you that it doesn't stop there? What if I told you that, before Barack Obama became president of the United States, there was actually another black man who ruled the world?

We usually associate him with paganism because he founded the land of Shinar/Babylon, but Nimrod, Ham's grandson, was also a black man, and he was the first ruler of the world.

Look at what it says in Genesis 10:8-10.

> *"Cush begot Nimrod; he began to be a mighty one on the earth. He was a mighty hunter before the Lord; therefore, it is said, 'Like Nimrod the mighty hunter before the Lord.' And the beginning of his kingdom was Babel, Erech, Accad, and Calneh, in the land of Shinar."*

This is the first time the word "kingdom" is used in scripture, and it refers to a black man. Before then, no form of government existed on earth. So the first kingdom on earth was run by a black man. That says a lot about what black men are able to accomplish when they put their minds together.

In Genesis 11, it's under Nimrod's rulership that the people begin to build the tower to reach heaven. Yet even though they were able to accomplish such an amazing feat, with their ingenuity and their ability to work together on one accord, because they had not fully trusted in God, he was forced to confuse their languages. Now granted, it wasn't what God wanted, but just think about what they did. Here you have hundreds or thousands of black people working so well together that God says their languages have to be confused or nothing they want to do will be impossible.

This flies in the face of the notion that black people can't work together. If we did it back then, surely, we can do it today.

CHAPTER 3

I Didn't Know They Were Black

One of my biggest frustrations with our European view of Christianity is when I turn on the television, and the cast of almost every single bible movie is all white. To be honest, that's the main reason why I stopped watching bible movies. I just can't continue to watch something that I know isn't true...especially when I know the producers are aware of the fact that their depiction isn't true as well. To me it just doesn't make sense why it's so hard to cast people of color in these roles of bible characters that we know were not white.

Even though scripture contradicts this Hollywood narrative, they continue to promote this false belief that the Bible is white.

It's gotten so bad that, because we're so accustomed to seeing Moses, and David, and Joseph, etc. depicted as white, that is the mental picture we associate with these individuals.

It also doesn't make it any better when we act like the color of these individuals doesn't matter. If it doesn't matter, then why not depict them as what they looked like in scripture? If it doesn't matter, why should you care if someone points out that they were black instead of white?

As Christians, and even society as a whole, we've been so conditioned, or dare I say brainwashed, that even when we see evidence in scripture that contradicts what we believe on this subject, many of us look right past it as if it doesn't matter. But the reality is that it does matter. If you've been lied to all your life, and now someone wants to point out the lie, you should want to know the truth. Not only should you want to know the truth, but you should be doing everything you can to expose the lie so that others might be enlightened as well.

When I look at the state of black America, I can't help but wonder how life might be different, if we as African Americans, knew that truth has been hidden from us for over 400 years. I wonder if we knew the truth that nobody wants us to know, if it would make a difference in how we saw ourselves, as well as one another.

They Were Really Black

When I look at scripture, it amazes me how many bible characters were black, yet very few people know or acknowledge that fact.

When we begin to talk about bible characters being black, we have to begin with our first parents, Adam and Eve. The Bible says in Genesis 2:7 that "God formed man of the dust of the ground..." That basically means man came from the dirt, and we all know that dirt is brown.

We also have to remember that two white people cannot produce a person of color. That is scientifically impossible. That means, if Adam and Eve were created as White in complexion, no people of color would exist. White people carry less amounts of melanin in their DNA, so they are unable to produce a person of color. On the other hand, because Adam and Eve were people of color, they could reproduce people of many shades of color, even White. We know this because two dark-skinned people can produce an Albino child.

Another example of blacks in scripture is in Genesis 37. In this chapter, Joseph is sold into slavery by his brothers. After initially being sold to the Midianites, he would then be sold to the Egyptians. Over time, because of his faithfulness in service, Joseph would rise to become the prime minister of Egypt. Decades later, a famine would hit the land of Canaan. During that time, Joseph's family is living in Canaan. Since they are also affected by the famine, Joseph's brothers travel to Egypt to buy grain. When they get there, they don't recognize Joseph. The reason they don't recognize him is because he wasn't white, as he's usually depicted.

In Exodus 1, the new Pharaoh makes a decree that all Hebrew baby boys be killed after they're born. Since Moses' mother doesn't want her son killed, she puts him in a basket and places the basket in the river.

Pharaoh's daughter eventually finds Moses in the river and raises him as her own son. Now, we know the Pharaoh's daughter was black because she was Egyptian. We then have to ask, "How could she pass Moses off as her own son if he was white and she was black?"

Later on, in Exodus 2, when Moses gets older, he flees to Midian after killing an Egyptian. When he gets there, he helps Jethro's daughters, who were being prevented from having access to a well by a group of shepherds. When they go home, they tell their father, Jethro, that an Egyptian delivered them from the hand of the shepherds.

In verse 19, it says,

> *"And they said, 'An Egyptian delivered us from the hand of the shepherds, and he also drew enough water for us and watered the flock."*

Why would they mistake Moses for an Egyptian if he was white?

Since his complexion was the same as everybody else's, they identified him by what he wore, instead of by how he looked?

It doesn't stop there because, by the time we get to chapter 4, God has called Moses to deliver the children of Israel out of Egypt. Unfortunately, Moses is afraid that if he tells the people that God called him to deliver them from Pharaoh, the people won't believe him. God gives him three miracles to prove to them that what he was saying was true. One of the miracles included turning his hand white.

In Exodus 4:6-7, it says,

> *"Furthermore the Lord said to him, 'Now put your hand in your bosom.' And he put his hand in his bosom, and when he took it out, behold, his hand was leprous, like snow. And He said, 'Put your hand in your bosom again.' So, he put his hand in his bosom again, and drew it out of his bosom, and behold, it was restored like his other flesh."*

If Moses' hand was already white, why would it need to be restored like his "other flesh?"

Remember, the purpose of the miracles was to convince the people that he'd been sent by God. That means the purpose of each miracle was to convince those who weren't convinced by the previous one.

That would suggest that this second miracle was to be more impressive than the first. But how could it be more impressive if Moses' hand was already white?

It was more impressive, not because his hand was already white, but because his hand was actually black. Therefore, Moses was black.

This is powerful because it means that the first five books of the Bible were written by a black man.

Just think about that...the first five books of the Bible were written by a black man.

That is amazing when you contemplate how important that is, and what it means to those who don't feel as though black people have contributed anything valuable to society.

In Numbers 12, when Moses' sister, Miriam, goes off on Moses for marrying an Ethiopian/Cushite woman, we're told that God strikes her with leprosy, causing her skin to turn white as snow.

In Numbers 12:9-10, it says,

> "So the anger of the Lord was aroused against them, and He departed. And when the cloud departed from above the tabernacle, suddenly Miriam became leprous, as white as snow."

If Miriam were already white, why would the text say that she became "white as snow?" It must have been because she wasn't white but black. Since her brother was black, would that not also be more proof that she was most likely black too?

This also dispels the notion that Miriam was upset at Moses because he married a black woman- which is what some people teach.

In the book *Old Testament Essays*, Peter J. Williams brings up this point when he says,

> "The woman from Cush was offensive to Miriam and Aaron because she was a black African woman. We stress here a black African woman because the Egyptian princess in whose house Moses grew up, was an African woman. ... The issue raised by Aaron, Miriam and also the narrator of this story at this point is not that of being anti-foreign, but anti-black. It is a racist issue."

So this notion that Miriam was upset at Moses because he married a black woman is not some far left conspiracy theory.

But how could she be upset that Moses' wife was black if Miriam herself was black? The reason Miriam was upset was because Moses married a woman who was not of the same faith; Zipporah was an Ethiopian, and Moses was a Hebrew. It's like if my sister was a Baptist, and I get upset with her because she marries a Catholic. It had nothing to do with the color of the person's skin.

Joshua, another prominent figure in the Bible, was also black. In Numbers 13:8, we're told that Joshua was from the tribe of Ephraim.

Ephraim was the youngest of Joseph's two sons with his Egyptian wife, Asenath. Ephraim would be the father of one of the twelve tribes of Israel. Since Joshua was of that tribe, that would mean he was black.

In 2 Samuel 12, King David has a son named Solomon by his wife, Bathsheba. In the Enhanced Strong's Lexicon, as well as the Strong's Concordance, the Hebrew for daughter is "Bath." So, Bathsheba literally means the "daughter of Sheba." So, then the question is, "Who was Sheba?"

In Genesis 10:7 it says,

> *"The sons of Cush were Seba, Havilah, Sabtah, Raamah, and Sabtechah; and the sons of Raamah were Sheba and Dedan."*

So, Sheba was a descendant of Cush. According to Gen.10:6, Cush was a descendant of Ham. We've already learned that Ham was the progenitor of black people. That means that Bathsheba, the daughter of Sheba, had to be black.

Scripture also tells us that, before Bathsheba married David, she was married to a man named Uriah the Hittite (2 Samuel 11:3-4, NKJV). The Hittites were the descendants of Heth. According to Genesis 10:15, Heth was a son of Canaan. Since we know that Canaan was black, Uriah the Hittite, would also have been black.

In 2 Kings 5, we find the story of Naaman. Naaman is the commander of the Syrian army, but he has leprosy. After finding out about Naaman's condition, his wife's servant girl tells him about a prophet named Elisha who can heal him of his leprosy.

Naaman then goes looking for Elisha. When he finds him, Elisha tells him to wash in the Jordan River seven times.

In 2 Kings 5:14, it says,

> *"So he went down and dipped seven times in the Jordan, according to the saying of the man of God; and his flesh was restored like the flesh of a child, and he was clean."*

When Miriam had leprosy, the Bible says that her skin turned white. That infers that her skin was previously another color. This would suggest that if Naaman also had leprosy and his skin turned white if it was restored to what it was before, it must have been a darker complexion.

When you continue in the story, Naaman wants to thank Elisha for healing him of leprosy. When he tries to give him a reward, Elisha doesn't take it. After Naaman leaves, Elisha's servant, Gehazi, chases him down and tells him that Elisha has changed his mind and that he actually wants something in return- even though he doesn't.

When Gehazi gets back, Elisha asks him where he's been. When he lies about his whereabouts, Elisha tells him that the leprosy of Naaman would cling to him and his descendants forever. 2 Kings 5:27 then says,

"...And he went out from his presence leprous, as white as snow."

So, if Gehazi's skin turned white, that means his skin could not have started off white. If it wasn't white to begin with, what color was it before?

Here we have Moses, Miriam, Naaman, and Gehazi, who were all either leprous or became leprous. In Naaman's case, his skin was restored. In Moses and Miriam's case, their hands turned leprous and then back to normal. Then in Gehazi's case, his skin was one complexion and turned another complexion (white) after being cursed. That leads me to believe that all four of these individuals were born with a dark complexion.

In Genesis 25:1, it says, "Abraham again took a wife, and her name was Keturah." Keturah is his second wife because his first wife Sarah had already died (Genesis 23:2). Abraham and Keturah would go on to have six sons: Zimran, Jokshan, Medan, Midian, Ishbak, and Shuah (Genesis 25:2, NKJV).

Their son Midian would become the father of the Midianites. According to Exodus 3:1, Moses' father-in-law, Jethro, was the priest of the Midianites. He was also the father of Moses' wife, Zipporah. That means that Zipporah was a Midianite. In Numbers 12:1, we're told that Zipporah was also an Ethiopian/Cushite. Cush is another name for Ethiopia. Since Ethiopians were black, Zipporah would have had to have also been black.

If Zipporah was black, then her father, Jethro, who was a Midianite, was also black. If he was black, then his father, Midian, was black. If Midian was black, then his father Abraham and Keturah were black as well.

We also know that Abraham's son, Ishmael, was black, because according to Genesis 21:9, his mother Hagar was an Egyptian. That means Abraham would have also been black.

But listen to what it says about his son, Ishmael, in Genesis 21:21. "He (Ishmael) dwelt in the Wilderness of Paran; and his mother took a wife for him from the land of Egypt.

If Ishmael's wife was from Egypt, that means she was also black. And Ishmael wasn't the only one who married a black woman. The Bible tells us that Esau had a black wife as well.

In Genesis 28:8-9, it says,

> *"Also Esau saw that the daughters of Canaan did not please his father Isaac. So, Esau went to Ishmael and took Mahalath the daughter of Ishmael, Abraham's son, the sister of Nebajoth, to be his wife in addition to the wives he had."*

Now, we just read that Ishmael's wife was black- which means that his daughter Mahalath had to be black as well. That means Esau also married a black woman.

In Genesis 38:2, it says that Judah's wife, Shua, was a Canaanite. When we turn over to Genesis 10:6, we see that Canaan is a descendant of Ham. Since we know that Ham was black, we know his son Canaan was black as well. If Canaan was black, then Judah's wife, Shua, who was a Canaanite, had to be black as well. That also means the tribe of Judah was black, but we'll talk more about that in a later chapter.

In Genesis 41:45, Joseph marries Potiphar's daughter Asenath. Potiphar was the king of Egypt. Egypt was full of black people, which means that Potiphar and Asenath were both black. Asenath and Joseph would go on to have two children, Manasseh and Ephraim. Manasseh and Ephraim, of course, would be black as well. Manasseh and Ephraim would also later become two of the twelve tribes of Israel.

We also know Joseph was black because, after his brothers sold him into slavery, when they went to Egypt years later during the famine, they didn't even recognize him. If he were white, should he not have stood out among all the black people in Egypt? So, we know Joseph was black.

Now, before we move on, we need to make sure we have a clear understanding of what the ancient Egyptians looked like back then. For some reason, their skin complexion has been debated for years. I really don't understand why, because first of all, when the Egyptians depicted themselves in paintings, they always painted themselves black.

Image via: (Mary Sabuda, "Copper Content of Ancient Egyptian Ink May Help Us (Literally) Piece Together Egyptian History," December 21, 2017, https://sciworthy.com/copper-content-of-ancient-egyptian-ink-may-help-us-literally-piece-together-egyptian-history/)

If they depicted themselves as being black, why would anyone insist that they were anything other than black? To be honest, besides the racist blackface caricatures of the 19th and 20th centuries, I don't know of any white person who would intentionally paint themselves black. It just doesn't make sense. It's obvious from the picture shown that the color white was available to them. So if the people of that time were white, why wouldn't they have also painted their skin white as well? The only logical reason is because they weren't white to begin with. This is why it's obvious that the ancient Egyptians were black.

So to say that the original Egyptians were anything but black, a person would have to either be disingenuous or just plain ignorant of history. Look at what history tells us about the complexion of the ancient Egyptians:

> *"The Ethiopians stain the world and depict a race of men steeped in darkness; less sun-burnt are the natives of India; the land of Egypt, flooded by the Nile, darkens bodies more mildly owing to the inundation of its fields: it is a country nearer to us, and its moderate climate imparts a medium tone."* (Astronomica 1977)

> *"the men of Egypt are mostly brown and black with a skinny desiccated look."* (Ammianus Marcellinus)

> *"Why are the Ethiopians and Egyptians bandy-legged? Is it because the bodies of living creatures become distorted by heat, like logs of wood when they become dry? The condition of their hair supports this theory; for it is curlier than that of other nations, and curliness is as it were crookedness of the hair."* (Physiognomics 1984)

> *"For it is plain to see that the Colchians are Egyptians; and what I say, I myself noted before I heard it from others. When it occurred to me, I inquired of both peoples; and the Colchians remembered the Egyptians better than the Egyptians remembered the Colchians; the Egyptians said that they considered the Colchians part of Sesostris' army. I myself guessed it, partly because they are black-skinned and woolly-haired; though that indeed counts for nothing, since other peoples are, too; but my better proof was that the Colchians and Egyptians and Ethiopians are the only nations that have from the first practised circumcision."* (Herodotus 1998)

History is clear that the ancient Egyptians were black. They were not, as some scholars or scientists like to insist, fair-skinned. They were not white. They were people with dark complexions.

The only reason modern Egyptians are not overwhelmingly dark in complexion is because for over 2800 years ancient Egypt was conquered and ruled by foreign invaders. When these invaders are white and come from places like Greece, and Rome, and Turkey, eventually, the darker complexions will become lighter. That is why, today, Egypt has become a melting pot of races and cultures.

In Genesis 11:31, it says that Abraham was from the land of Ur of the Chaldeans. Ur was a city in southern Mesopotamia, in what today is modern-day Iraq. Ur was also located on what was considered North Africa. If you look at a historical map of the area we call the Middle East, you will notice that Ur is east of Canaan, near Babylon. This entire area was inhabited by black people. Therefore, it is safe to say that they were also black.

When we get to the New Testament, we see the same thing we saw in the Old Testament, Bible characters who've always been depicted in society as being white, when in actuality, they were black.

A perfect example is Paul. Paul is often assumed to be white, even though the scriptures are clear that Paul was black. One reason for this misconception is that Paul was a Roman citizen who was born in Tarsus, and Tarsus is in Turkey. Since Turkey and Rome are European countries, people have assumed that Paul must have been white. However, the Bible makes it clear that Paul could not have been white.

In Acts 21, Paul has been arrested for bringing Gentiles into the temples and allegedly teaching doctrines that were in contradiction to the laws of the people. After a huge commotion, he is eventually taken before the commander of the Jerusalem army.

In verse 37-39, it says,

"Then as Paul was about to be led into the barracks, he said to the commander, 'May I speak to you?' He (commander) replied, 'Can you speak Greek? Are you not the Egyptian who some time ago stirred up a rebellion and led the four thousand assassins out into the wilderness?' But Paul said, 'I am a Jew from Tarsus, in Cilicia, a citizen of no mean city; and I implore you, permit me to speak to the people.'"

After being brought before the commander, Paul is mistaken for an Egyptian. Why would he be mistaken for an Egyptian if he was white? Since we know that Egyptians were black, the only way he could have been mistaken for an Egyptian is if he was also black.

So, then the question becomes, "How could Paul be from Tarsus, be a Roman citizen, yet still be black?" Unfortunately, there is no precise answer to that question.

What we do know is that he was a Jew (Philemon 3:5, NKJV), and his father was a Jew (Acts 23:6, NKJV). We also know that according to Acts 21:37, he looked like an Egyptian, and Egyptians were black.

It is possible that, at some point, his mother and father moved to Rome. While in Rome, Paul may have been born. That would make him a Roman citizen by birth. It is just like if someone from Mexico moved to the United States and had a child. Since their parents were Mexican, the child would have Mexican heritage due to the fact that their parents were from Mexico. However, they would be considered a citizen of the United States due to the fact that they were born in this country.

It's also possible that Paul was born in Rome, but after his birth, his parents moved to Tarsus. That could be the reason why the Bible mentions that he was a Roman citizen but was also from Tarsus. This actually makes a lot of sense because, even though I was born in Wilmington, DE, I was raised in Washington, D.C. So, when people ask where I am from, I usually say I'm from D.C. When they ask where I was born, I say that I was born in Delaware.

So, despite the fact that Paul was a Roman citizen from Tarsus, it doesn't take away from the fact that he was black.

CHAPTER 4

The Real Gentiles

If you're a Christian, then you know that Christians have always been taught that there are two groups of people in scripture- there are Jews, and there are Gentiles. God's chosen people are Jews, while everybody else is a Gentile. No matter how long we've been in the church, no matter what denomination we were raised in, we've all been led to believe that Gentiles are non-Jews.

In fact, even in the Merriam-Webster dictionary, a "Gentile" is defined as a person of a non-Jewish nation or faith. So, this is not some belief that started yesterday. This has always been the accepted norm.

But what if I told you that if you look from Genesis to Revelation, you will not find one scripture that validates this false teaching? What if I told you that, according to scripture, a Gentile is somebody entirely different?

Now let me be clear; this chapter is going to be very uncomfortable for most readers. It's going to be uncomfortable because the truth is uncomfortable. But understand that, in no way do I share this information to demean, disparage, or belittle any person or people group. I present this for the sole purpose of educating the reader as to the real identity of the Gentiles. In Ephesians 4:25, Paul says,

> "Therefore, putting away lying, 'Let each one of you speak the truth with his neighbor, for we are members one of another.'"

Paul, the writer of Ephesians, admonishes us to put away falsehoods and to speak the truth with our neighbors because we are all part of one another, or the same body. I take that to mean that we should not lie, nor withhold the truth from our neighbor. As people of color, we are often hesitant to bring up certain topics, or express our true feelings, in order not to offend anyone. And although my intention is not to offend, as

Paul says in Ephesians 4:15, we must still speak the truth in love.

Scripture tells us that everybody on the earth is a descendant of one of Noah's three sons: Shem, Ham, and Japheth. From these three sons, the entire world was populated.

In Genesis 9:18-19, it says,

> *"Now the sons of Noah who went out of the ark were Shem, Ham, and Japheth. And Ham was the father of Canaan. These three were the sons of Noah, and from these the whole earth was populated."*

When we get to Genesis 10, we find the genealogy of these three sons. This section is often referred to as the Table of Nations because all the people of the earth descended from one of these three sons. Japheth's people settled north of Israel in the area we call Europe. Ham's people settled in the area we know as Africa. Shem's line would eventually settle in the area we now call the Middle East. From there, all the nations would be populated.

In Genesis 10:1-4, it says,

> *"Now this is the genealogy of the sons of Noah: Shem, Ham, and Japheth. And sons were born to them after the flood. The sons of Japheth were Gomer, Magog, Madai, Javan, Tubal, Meshech, and Tiras. The sons of Gomer were Ashkenaz, Riphath, and Togarmah. The sons of Javan were Elishah, Tarshish, Kittim, and Dodanim."*

These names correlate with the names and people of the specific geographical regions in the ancient world, some of whom would interact with the people of Israel on different occasions. After they're mentioned in Genesis 10, they're rarely mentioned in scripture, specifically in the Old Testament. When they are mentioned, they are in opposition to the people of God. (Ezekiel 38:2, NKJV), Tarshish (Genesis 10:4; Psalm 72:10; Ezekiel 38:13) and Kittim (Genesis 10:4; Numbers 24:24; Daniel 11:30).

Of the sons of Japheth, Gomer founded the Celts. According to history.com, *"The Celts were a collection of tribes with origins in central Europe that shared a similar language, religious beliefs, traditions, and culture. It's believed that the Celtic culture started to evolve as early as 1200 B.C. The Celts spread throughout western Europe – including Britain, Ireland, France, and Spain – via migration. Their legacy remains most prominent in Ireland and Great*

Britain, where traces of their language and culture are still prominent today."

The area settled by Japheth's second son, Magog, is a topic of dispute among some scholars. While some believe he settled in Lydia, which is now the country known as Turkey, others believe he settled in Russia. Madai, Japheth's third son, means "Middle land," and it is suggested that Madai is the ancestor of the Medians (Medes), which was south of the Caspian Sea. Japheth's fourth son, Javan, was said to be the forefather of the Greeks, most particularly of the Ionians, one of the first Greek nations. The Ionians dwelt in the land of Iona. Javan was the term used in the Bible referring to Greece.

Tubal is said to be the ancestor of the Italians, Spanish, and Caucasian Iberians. Meshech is said to be the ancestor of several nations like the Mosocheni, Illyrians, Georgians, Caucasians, Armenians. Japheth's seventh son, Tiras, has been linked to the Thracians, the Agathyrsi, the tribes of the Taurus mountain region, and the maritime Tyrrheni. Ashkenaz, the son of Gomer, Japheth's grandson, would settle the area known as Germany. (Ashkenaz will make another appearance in a later chapter.) Riphath, Gomer's second son, has been identified by the Jewish historian Josephus with the Paphlagonians. Paphlagonia is in northeast Turkey by the Black Sea. Gomer's third son, Togarmah, was the ancestor of peoples in the Caucasus mountains and western Asia.

When you look at a map of the areas these sons and grandsons founded, the first thing you notice is that all of these areas are in Europe. None of Japheth's sons or grandsons settled in any of the African countries. This is why it's almost universally understood that Europeans are the descendants of Japheth.

At this time, you may be wondering how Noah could have a white son if we already learned that Ham was black. What science tells us is that two dark-skinned people can, and have, produced children that had a fair complexion, even white. A perfect example is the albino. It is genetically impossible for two white people to produce dark-skinned children. Therefore, Noah and his wife could have had Ham, who we know were black, and still have Japheth, who was white. Ham and Japheth could have also both been black, while Japheth turned white at a later time. We just don't know.

Now before we move on, it's important to point out how the lineage of Noah's other two sons ends.

> *In regards to the lineage of Ham, Genesis 10:6 says,*
> *"The sons of Ham were Cush, Mizraim, Put, and Canaan."*

Verses 7–19 then continue on with the lineage of Ham. When you get to verse 20, it says,

> *"These were the sons of Ham, according to their families, according to their languages, in their lands and in their nations."*

In reference to Shem's lineage, verse 21 says, "And children were born also to Shem, the father of all the children of Eber, the brother of Japheth the elder." It then continues with the lineage of Shem. In verse 31, it says, "These were the sons of Shem, according to their families, according to their languages, in their lands, according to their nations."

In both the line of Ham and the line of Shem, the writer concludes each lineage by stating that "these were the sons of Ham/Shem according to their families, languages, lands, and nations."

When you look back at the line of Japheth, the closing of his lineage ends differently from his other two brothers.

In Genesis 10:2-4, it says, "The sons of Japheth were Gomer, Magog, Madai, Javan, Tubal, Meshech, and Tiras. The sons of Gomer were Ashkenaz, Riphath, and Togarmah. The sons of Javan were Elishah, Tarshish, Kittim, and Dodanim." This is equivalent to what we see in the lineage of the other two brothers. But, notice what it says in verse 5 to close Japheth's lineage.

> *"(From these the coastland peoples of the Gentiles were separated into their lands, everyone according to his language, according to their families, into their nations.)"*

Now, this is interesting because, instead of ending Japheth's lineage like he ended Ham's and Shem's, the writer says, "from these the coastland peoples of the Gentiles were separated into their lands, everyone according to his language, according to their families, into their nations."

The first question we have to ask is, "Who are 'these'?" These would have to be the names we just read in verses 2-4.

Now, as I said before, we've always been taught that the Gentiles are those of us of "non-Jewish faith." But according to the Bible, the Gentiles are Gomer, Magog, Javan, Tubal, etc., the descendants of Japheth. In other words, the Gentiles are those who descended from European nations.

I know you're thinking to yourself, "What in the world?" I know, right!

But when you think about it, it makes sense. The Gentiles couldn't be all those who are "non-Jews" because the term Gentiles is used before the "Jewish race" was even established. If the first "Jew" didn't come into existence for another 1500-2000 years, how could the term "Gentile" refer to non-Jews?

Also, according to scripture, Paul was the "apostle to the Gentiles." He was not the apostle to the Jews. He was the apostle to the Gentiles. That means he was called specifically to share the Gospel with the Gentiles.

In Romans 11:13, Paul says,

> "For I speak to you Gentiles; inasmuch as I am an apostle to the Gentiles, I magnify my ministry."

In Ephesians 3:8, he says, "To me, who am less than the least of all the saints, this grace was given, that I should preach among the Gentiles the unsearchable riches of Christ." Again, scripture is clear that Paul was the apostle to the Gentiles.

So, now the question has to be asked, "Where did Paul share the Gospel?" If we can find the answer to that, we can determine who the Gentiles are.

When you look through the books of Acts, Romans, Galatians, Ephesians, Philippians, etc., the one thing that is clear is that Paul's missionary journeys led him to one geographical area. That area was Europe. Paul did not preach the gospel in Africa. He went to Athens, which was in Greece. He went to Corinth, which was also in Greece. He went to Iconium and Tarsus, which were in Turkey. He went to Malta, which was in Italy. He went to Spain and Rome. Each one of his missionary journeys were in Europe. Nowhere in scripture does it mention Paul preaching to Gentiles in Africa. We know the apostles went to Africa, but as the apostle to the Gentiles, the scriptures never mention Paul going to Africa.

If he's the apostle to the Gentiles, and as we've been taught, the Gentiles are non-Jews, why didn't he find any in Africa? You would think that, since he was the apostle to the Gentiles, he would preach to the Gentiles wherever they were. But, for some reason, he only goes to Europe. I wonder why that is. Could it be that the reason he only went to Europe is because the Gentiles were Europeans? What other explanation is there? If the descendants of Japheth inhabited the European countries, and Genesis 10:5 says that, from Japheth's line, "the coastland peoples of the Gentiles were separated into their lands," who else could the Gentiles be?

When Jesus was arrested in the Garden of Gethsemane, He was arrested by Roman soldiers. When He died, it was by crucifixion, which was the Roman form of putting someone to death. Most Christians will acknowledge that the Romans put Jesus to death. Yet when Jesus describes those responsible for His death, He doesn't use the term "Romans," He uses the term "Gentiles."

In Matthew 20:17-19, it says, "Now Jesus, going up to Jerusalem, took the twelve disciples aside on the road and said to them, 'Behold, we are going up to Jerusalem, and the Son of Man will be betrayed to the chief priests and to the scribes; and they will condemn Him to death, and deliver Him to the Gentiles to mock and to scourge and to crucify. And the third day He will rise again."

Why would Jesus use the term "Gentiles" when it's clear that it was the Romans that crucified Him? Could it have been that Jesus saw Romans and Gentiles as being one and the same? Could it be that the Romans were called Gentiles because they were of European descent?

In Matthew 10:6, when Jesus sends out the apostles, He tells them to first go share the good news with the lost sheep of Israel. After going to the lost sheep of Israel, they were then to go to the Gentiles. How were the disciples supposed to know who was, and who was not a Gentile? Could it be that they knew because of the color of their skin?

In Matthew 10:5-6, it says,

> *"These twelve Jesus sent out and commanded them, saying: 'Do not go into the way of the Gentiles, and do not enter a city of the Samaritans. But go rather to the lost sheep of the house of Israel."*

So, Jesus sends out the Twelve, He tells them not to go to the Gentiles, but to first go to the lost sheep of Israel." We now have to ask, "Where did they go?" Did they look for lost sheep in Europe? No. They began in Israel, which was considered North Africa. That means all of the lost sheep had to have been in North Africa. That also means there were no lost sheep in Europe. The reason there were no lost sheep in Europe is because the Gentiles were in Europe.

I know that's hard to swallow because we've been conditioned to believe that Gentiles are non-Jews. But, unfortunately, scripture doesn't back that up. When we look at scripture, it tells us something completely different. In fact, we probably don't even know where we were first taught that Gentiles are non-Jews. It's just a false teaching that has been passed down from church to church, but few people ever questioned it. Too often, we accept what is passed down without going back to research for ourselves to find out if what we've been taught was true.

In Acts 17:11, Paul admonishes the believers in Berea because they didn't just take what he said at face value but went back and studied the scriptures for themselves, to see if what he said was true. It is our responsibility as believers to do the same. We must search the scriptures for ourselves and stop believing everything we hear from the pulpit.

Now, as always, there will be some who will read this chapter and think that I am a racist, or that I believe that white people can't be saved.

Let me be clear: THAT IS ABSOLUTELY NOT TRUE.

Paul says in Galatians 3:28, that "There is neither Jew nor Gentile, neither slave nor free, nor is there male nor female; for you are all one in Christ Jesus (NIV)." So, there is no difference between Jews and Gentiles, when it comes to salvation because we all need Jesus.

There will be white people saved, just like there will be black people saved. There will also be white people lost, just like there will be black people lost. Their salvation will be determined by whether or not they accepted Christ as Savior. So this is not about trying to justify a hatred toward white people or saying that white people won't be saved. I have to make this clear because there are groups that teach that white people won't be saved. The Bible doesn't teach that. There are countless scriptures that prove otherwise (John 3:16; Isaiah 49:6; Acts 10:45; Acts 11:1; Acts 11:18; Acts 13:47-48; Romans 11:11; Ephesians 3:4-6).

In fact, in Ephesians 3, Paul says the Gentiles, who accept Christ, will be fellow heirs and partakers of the same promise. So, this is not an attempt to say that whites won't make it to heaven. This is about unmasking the truth about black people in the Bible that's been hidden for so long.

And I use the phrase "unmasking the truth" because I truly believe this has been hidden intentionally. With all the white theologians and scholars who write commentaries, Bible dictionaries, and all kinds of other sources for biblical study, I refuse to believe none of them recognized that Gentiles were Europeans.

I believe that there are many white bible scholars who are aware that, according to scripture, white people are Gentiles, but because it makes them look bad, they refuse to admit it. But, the Bible says that, eventually, those who lied to God's people to make themselves look better, will receive the just penalty for their sins (Isaiah 42:1-3, NKJV).

CHAPTER 5

The Black Man's Book

In the last several years, there has been a consistent trend of black people leaving Christianity. One of the reasons is because young people are beginning to grow weary with organized religion. More and more of them have become discontent with religion, in general, because they don't see how organized religion is doing anything to impact their world. They're looking for a faith that makes sense for the world they see around them. They want to know how religion relates to race, ethnicity, and societal injustices.

Christianity is probably taking the biggest hit because many of us, as African Americans, are succumbing to the misnomer that Christianity is a white man's religion. More and more black people are starting to think that Christianity was created by white people for white people. They're asking questions like, "If Christianity is for everyone, why does the Bible endorse this country's first sin? Why doesn't Jesus look anything like me? Why is He always depicted as being of European descent? Wasn't Christianity the tool white people used to keep our ancestors enslaved?"

The reality is that there are a lot of people who believe black people weren't Christians before they came to this country. They believe that, before white people came and kidnapped us, we were kings and queens in Africa. It also doesn't help that the images they see in the media, politics, and the churches themselves, are a contradiction of what Christ taught.

As a result, black people are leaving because they want to worship something that is welcoming of black people. That's why many are turning to Egyptology, Islam, African witchcraft, and even atheism. They just don't see how Christianity relates to their everyday lives.

What's important to understand is that, yes, black people were enslaved. We also know that white people played a major part in these atrocities. Many did use the Bible to make blacks feel like being slaves was who we were always meant to be. But, what also has to be understood is that black people are not Christians today because of slavery. Black people are Christians because Christianity began in Africa. In fact, the truth is that white people got their theology from Africans, not the other way around. And, I know we've been taught to believe that it was the white missionaries that brought the gospel to Africa, but that would be the furthest thing from the truth. The gospel was in Africa over a thousand years before the first missionary came to the continent.

In Acts 1, we're told that the disciples met in an upper room after the death of Jesus. This was during the Jewish feast of Passover. During this holiday, Jews from all over the then-known-world would come to Jerusalem to celebrate the feast. While the disciples were meeting, the Holy Spirit came upon them, and they began to speak in unknown tongues, to the Jews gathered there.

In Acts 2:9-10, it names the places in which these Jews were visiting from. It says there were

"Parthians and Medes and Elamites, those dwelling in Mesopotamia, Judea and Cappadocia, Pontus and Asia. Phrygia and Pamphylia, Egypt and the parts of Libya adjoining Cyrene..."

What most people don't realize is that half of the places mentioned in this verse are in Africa. Mesopotamia is modern-day Iraq, which is in what was considered North Africa. Judea, which is in Jerusalem, was also in North Africa. Libya, Egypt, and Cyrene are also in Africa.

That means, when the disciples preached from Jerusalem (North Africa) to the Jews from these other countries, these Jews received the Gospel over a thousand years before the first western missionary stepped foot onto the continent.

If the Jews, who were gathered there, went back to their respective homes in Libya, Egypt, Cyrene, etc., and shared the gospel, then those countries also received the gospel over a thousand years prior to the white missionaries bringing it over. That means it is impossible for Europeans to have introduced the gospel to Africa.

If we look further at scripture, we find more proof that the Gospel was in Africa before the white missionaries got there in the 19th century.

In Acts 8, we find the story of the Ethiopian Eunuch. In the story,

Phillip is told by an Angel of the Lord to go down a desert road. While going down the road, he comes across the Ethiopian eunuch who's traveling home from Jerusalem. He's in his chariot reading the scroll of the prophet Isaiah when he's told to overtake the chariot. When he catches up to the chariot, he hears the eunuch reading from the prophet Isaiah. Philip then asks him if he understands what he's reading. The eunuch says, "How can I understand unless someone teaches me?" Philip then begins to explain to him the scriptures concerning Jesus Christ. So, the eunuch also learned about the Gospel before the white missionaries arrived.

In the same book, in Acts 13:1, we're introduced to a man called Simeon, a prophet and a teacher, who was called Niger. Niger literally means "dark skin." He was one of the early Christians that helped spread the gospel.

In the same verse, it talks about Lucius of Cyrene, who was also a prophet and teacher. Cyrene is located in Libya, and Libya is in Africa.

So, this whole notion that Europeans brought the Gospel to Africa, and that Christianity is a white man's religion, and that the Bible was given to our ancestors to keep us in slavery- is nothing but a lie.

As a matter of fact, if there's any group of people that should be Christians, it should be black people because the birthplace of Christianity was in Africa. That's why Africa has the largest number of Christians in the world at over 631 million. Latin America is second with 601 million. Europe is in third place, with 571 million. That means at least 1.2 of the 2.3 billion Christians in the world, or more than half, are people of color. That doesn't include the Christians in other countries that have a large number of people of color (JP Mauro, "Africa overtakes Latin America for the highest Christian population," July 24, 2018, accessed September 14, 2020).

What we usually don't think about, when it comes to black representation in Christianity, is the fact that some of the early church fathers were black. Tertullian, who was often called "the founder of Western Theology," was from a place called Carthage. Carthage is now called Tunisia, and it is located in North Africa. Tertullian is responsible for inventing the term "Trinity." Origen of Alexandria was also an early church father. Alexandria is in Egypt. Origen is credited for writing "On the First Principles," which systematically laid out principles for Christian Theology. It would become foundational for theological writings that came after it. Augustine of Hippo was another black early church father. His two books, "The City of God," and "On Christian Doctrine" are considered to be important works that influenced Western Christianity and Western philosophy. Augustine was from Hippo Regius, which was in North Africa.

The oldest church in the world is known as the Dura-Europos church, or Dura-Europos house church. It is one of the earliest known Christian churches in the world, and it was located in Syria, which was in North Africa. The Dura-Europos church was initially a typical domestic house before it was converted for worship. It dates sometime between 233AD and 256AD (Churchpop Editor, "1,782 Years Old: Inside the Oldest Church in the World," June 22, 2015, accessed September 14, 2020)

Did you know that, when you look at scripture, the European countries of Rome and Greece are both mentioned less than 20 times, but Ethiopia, Canaan, and Egypt (all Hamitic countries with black people) are mentioned thousands of times?

Therefore, Christianity is not a "white man's religion," and the Bible is not a "white man's book. If it's anybody's book, and if it's anybody's religion, it's the black man's. And, I know that's not what we've been taught, but it's true. When we look at the proof, it only leads to one conclusion. Without black people there is no Christianity.

It's important for us to understand this, because as a people, we've been oppressed, and demeaned, and told that we're 3/5 of a man, so we need to know that we are somebody… it's called the power of representation.

After winning an award for her role in the movie "12 Years a Slave," Kenyan actress Lupita Nyong'o shot to fame, in the interviews that followed, she repeatedly talked about feeling inferior as a young woman because all the images of beauty she saw around her were of lighter-skinned women. And, it was only after she saw the fashion world embrace Sudanese model Alek Wek that she realized that black could be beautiful as well.

When you've been told, or when you've been led to believe that nobody in scripture looks like you, you look for other venues to find representation. That's one of the main reasons why black people are leaving the church. That's why black men are turning to Islam. That's why our young people look up to entertainers, and athletes, because they don't see any other representation.

But, when they can read scripture and know that the Moses who led

God's people out of Israel, and the Joseph who was second in charge over all of Egypt- when they can read about people like that, and know that those individuals looked just like them, it enables them to believe that, with God, anything is possible.

Marcus Garvey once said, "If we as a people realized the greatness from which we came, we would be less likely to DISRESPECT OURSELVES."

I honestly believe that, if we knew who we were and where we came from, we would be in a better place as a people than where we are now.

CHAPTER 6

Identity Theft

Have you ever wondered why the wealth gap between a typical white family is ten times greater than a typical black family? Have you ever wondered why blacks are 1.3x more likely to be unarmed than white people, but 3x more likely to be killed by police (Sinyangwe, "Mapping Police Violence," accessed on September 1, 2020)?

Have you ever wondered why, whether armed or unarmed, blacks are 2.5 times more likely as whites to be shot and killed by police- despite the fact that African Americans only make up 13 percent of the population (Willem Roper, "Black Americans 2.5X More Likely Than Whites to Be Killed By Police," June 2, 2020, https://www.statista.com/chart/21872/map-of-police-violence-against-black-americans/)?

Have you ever wondered why in 99% of neighborhoods in the United States, black boys earn less in adulthood than white boys who grow up in families with a comparable income ("Racial Disparities in Income Mobility Persist, Especially for Men,' Opportunity Insights, accessed on Sept.1, 2020, https://opportunityinsights.org/race/)?

Have you ever wondered why black people are incarcerated at a rate of more than five times the rate of whites? Have you ever wondered why black children are more likely to be raised in single-parent homes than white children (Ashley Nellis, "The Color of Justice: Racial and Ethnic Disparity in State Prisons," June 14, 2016, https://www.sentencingproject.org/publications/color-of-justice-racial-and-ethnic-disparity-in-state-prisons/)?

Have you ever wondered why African Americans score lower than white Americans on vocabulary, reading, and math tests, as well as on tests that claim to measure scholastic aptitude and intelligence("Christopher Jencks, "The Black-White Test Score Gap: Why It Persists and What Can Be Done," March 1, 1998, https://www.brookings.edu/articles/

the-black-white-test-score-gap-why-it-persists-and-what-can-be-done/)?

Have you ever wondered why our heritage and our history aren't taught in school- and if it is, it always begins in 1619, as if black people didn't exist before slavery?

The answer to these questions is part of what I believe is the biggest coverup ever known to man. I call it identity theft.

In Wikipedia, it's described as

> *"the deliberate use of someone else's identity, usually as a way to gain some sort of financial advantage or to obtain credit and other benefits in another person's name. It usually occurs when that individual uses another person's personally identifying information like their name, or their social security number, or their credit card number. The person whose identity has been assumed is then at a disadvantage because they're the one who ends up suffering the consequences of the perpetrator's actions."*

I believe African Americans have been the victims of the biggest identity theft in history. They've had their identities stolen from them and are now suffering due to the consequences of their perpetrators' actions. What makes it even worse is that the majority of them don't even know it.

In chapter 2, we learned that Ham was the ancestor of black people. In chapter 4, we learned that Japheth was the progenitor of white people. We will now look at the lineage of Noah's other son, Shem. The lineage of Shem is important because it is the line in which the Hebrew people would come from. The Hebrews, of course, were God's chosen people. They were the ones God told to be witnesses to the other nations. They were the ones He delivered from the hand of Pharaoh. They were the ones He promised would be the head and not the tail. They were the ones He delivered time and time again even after they got themselves into unfortunate circumstances of their own doing.

To find out exactly which people descended from the line of Shem, we will look at the Table of Nations in Genesis 10.

In Genesis 10:21-22, it says,

> *"And children were born also to Shem, the father of all the children of Eber, the brother of Japheth the elder. The sons of Shem were Elam, Asshur, Arphaxad, Lud, and Aram."*

In Gen.11:10 it says, "This is the genealogy of Shem: Shem was one hundred years old, and begot Arphaxad two years after the flood. After he begot Arphaxad, Shem lived five hundred years and begot sons and daughters." The scriptures continue by giving the descendants of Shem. In verse 26 it says, "Now Terah lived seventy years, and begot Abram, Nahor, and Haran."

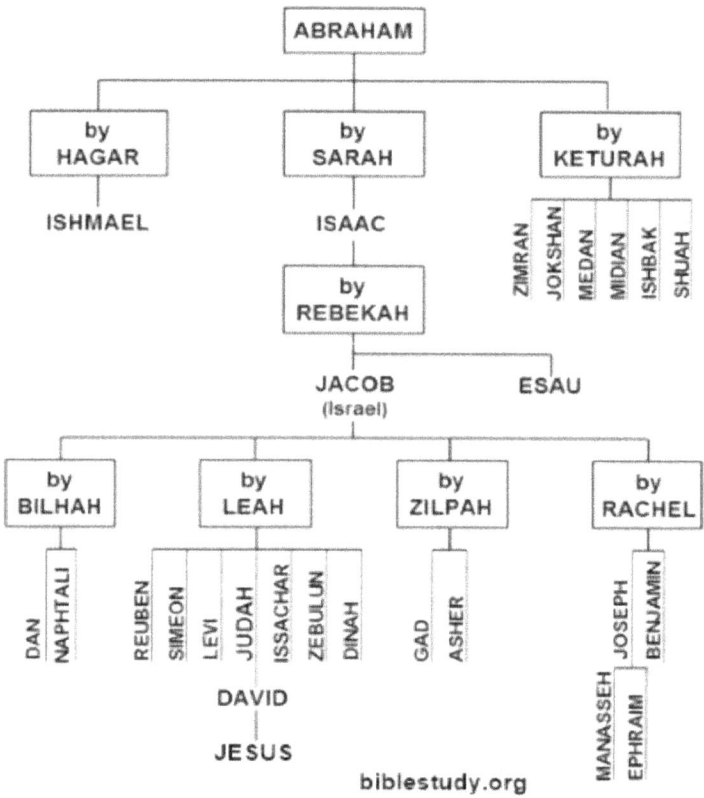

That means Abram, who would later become Abraham, was a descendant of Shem. Abraham was the father of the Hebrews. In verse 21, it says that Shem was "the father of the children of Eber." Eber is the eponymous ancestor of the Hebrews. In other words, Eber is where we get the term "Hebrews" from. The name Eber means to "pass through" or "cross over" and was indicative of Abraham and his descendants, Isaac and Jacob, who were nomads that would travel or pass through many lands on their nomadic journey. Jacob, Abraham's grandson, would have his name changed to Israel, and his twelve sons would become the twelve tribes of Israel. They would also be called Hebrews. Although Abram was the first person in the Bible called a Hebrew (Genesis 14:13, NKJV).

In chapter 3, we learned that Jacob's grandsons, Manasseh and Ephraim, the sons of Jacob's son Joseph, were black because Joseph was black. That means the tribe of Joseph was black.

Since the tribe of Joseph was black, his brother Benjamin would have had to be black as well since they both had the same mother, Rachel. This would mean that the tribe of Benjamin was also black. That would explain why Paul, who was from the tribe of Benjamin (Romans 11:1, NKJV), was mistaken for an Egyptian in Acts 21:38.

We could also assume that the tribe of Dan was black as well because the Bible says in Judges 16:13 that Samson, whose father was from the tribe of Dan, had dreadlocks. And, although there are more and more white people getting dreadlocks today, I don't know that too many of them had dreadlocks back then.

If we assume that Dan was black, it would also mean that the tribe of Naphtali was black as well, because in Genesis 30:6-8, it tells us they both had the same mother, Bilhah.

The tribe of Levi would also have been black because Moses was a Levite, and in Exodus 2, he's also mistaken for an Egyptian. If Levi was black, then Reuben, Simeon, Issachar, Judah, Zebulun, and Dinah had to black as well because they all had Leah as their mother.

When looking just at the scriptural evidence, it is obvious that at least ten of the twelve tribes were black. They weren't white. They weren't olive complexioned. They were black.

These twelve tribes were all descendants of Abraham, who was a descendant of Arphaxad. Since at least ten of the tribes were black, it is safe to assume that not only were the other two black, but Arphaxad was black as well. But to be sure, let's take a look at Shem's other sons, because according to Genesis 10:22, Arphaxad was only one of Shem's five sons.

Shem had another son named Asshur. The name "Asshur" means black in Hebrew, according to Strong's Concordance #806. That means we can assume his complexion was black as well.

You see, in the Bible, a name can describe a person's characteristics or their circumstances. When God told Abraham, who was 100-years-old at the time, that his 90-year-old wife would give birth to a son, Abraham and Sarah laughed. Sarah went on to give birth to a son named Isaac, which literally means "laughter" in Hebrew. Isaac would grow up and have twin sons. The first son was named Esau, which means "hairy" in Hebrew. Isaac named him that because of how hairy Esau was at birth. The second of the twin sons was born grasping at Esau's heel, and because of that, he was given the name Jacob, which means "that supplants" in Hebrew. True to his name, Jacob would go on to rob his older brother Esau of their father's blessing of the firstborn. As a result, Jacob would go on to wrestle with God and be renamed Israel, which in Hebrew means "wrestles with God."

So, there's precedent when it comes to a person's name meaning something. That's why we can safely assume that Asshur, whose name means black, was also black.

Shem had another son Elam who was the father of the Elamites. When we look at depictions of the Elamites, it is clear that they, too, were black. Their skin was dark. They had black curly hair. They looked like what black people look like today.

Palace of Ashurbanipal - Deporting the people of the Elamite city of Din Sharri - 645 B.C.

So, if Asshur, Elam, and Arphaxad were all black, it's most likely that all of his children were black. If all of them were black, then Shem was definitely black because two white people can't make a black child.

Windsor verifies this in his book *From Babylon to Timbuktu* when he states that,

> *"The parts of the earth inhabited by the children of Shem were: parts of the territory of Assyria and Elam (Persia) east of the Tigris River, the eastern part of Syria, and parts of the Arabian peninsula. All the children of Shem were black (Windsor 1969)."*

So, everything we've seen so far points to the fact that Noah's first son, Shem, was a black man. That means the son in which the lineage of the Hebrews would eventually come from was black. Take a moment and let that sink in... That is mind-blowing because it means that the children of Israel, God's chosen people, were black. It means that the slaves who were in Egypt for 400 years were black. It means that the people who crossed the Red Sea, on dry land, were black.

As a matter of fact, the descendants of Ham, and the descendants of Shem/Hebrews were indistinguishable by color. That's why Paul, Moses, and Joseph, who were all Hebrews, were all mistaken for Egyptians- because the Hebrews were black. There's even more evidence to this fact when we look at the Old Testament regulations that were given specifically to the Hebrews.

In the Book of Leviticus, Moses lists the ceremonial laws that governed the children of Israel. In chapter 13, he outlines the law regarding how a person with leprosy was to be treated.

In verses 2–5, it says,

> "When a man has on the skin of his body a swelling, a scab, or a bright spot, and it becomes on the skin of his body like a leprous sore, then he shall be brought to Aaron the priest or to one of his sons the priests. The priest shall examine the sore on the skin of the body; and if the hair on the sore has turned white, and the sore appears to be deeper than the skin of his body, it is a leprous sore. Then the priest shall examine him, and pronounce him unclean. But if the bright spot is white on the skin of his body, and does not appear to be deeper than the skin, and its hair has not turned white, then the priest shall isolate the one who has the sore seven days."

In verses 9-13, it says,

> "When the leprous sore is on a person, then he shall be brought to the priest. And the priest shall examine him; and indeed if the swelling on the skin is white, and it has turned the hair white, and there is a spot of raw flesh in the swelling, it is an old leprosy on the skin of his body. The priest shall pronounce him unclean, and shall not isolate him, for he is unclean.
>
> Moreover, if leprosy breaks out all over the skin, and the leprosy covers all the skin of the one who has the sore, from his head to his foot, wherever the priest looks, then the priest shall consider; and indeed if the leprosy has covered all his body, he shall pronounce him clean who has the sore. It has all turned white. He is clean."

What stands out in this group of texts is that one of the determining factors of whether or not a person had leprosy or not was if their skin, or hair, turned white. It would have been almost impossible for the priest to examine the individual and to determine if they had leprosy if their skin was already white. The only way for the priest to tell was is if the person's skin was a complexion other than white. If that is the case, then the ceremonial laws that were written to the children of Israel were written to people of color.

If you remember in chapter 3, we talked about how Naaman had leprosy, and after he dipped in the Jordan River seven times, his skin was restored. If his skin turned white as a result of his leprosy but was then restored, it had to have started off another complexion. From what we have learned so far, that complexion had to have been black.

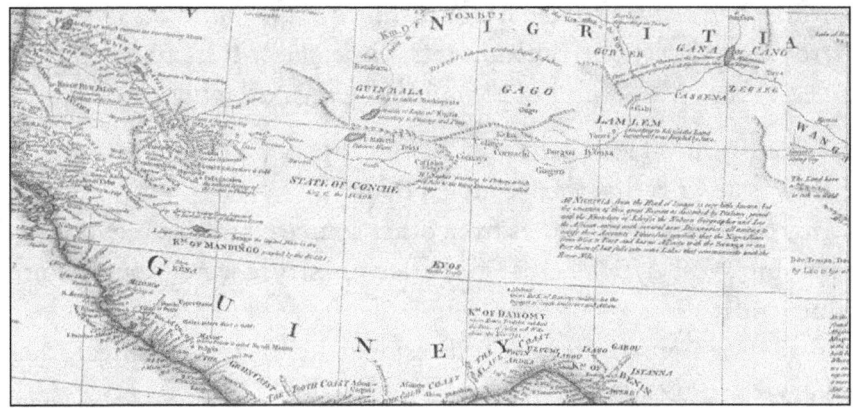

Image via: (1766: French Map Shows Negroland As "Populated By Jews," blackhistoryinthebible.org, accessed on Sept.1, 2020, https://www.blackhistoryinthebible.com/category/maps/)

Yet the proof for the Hebrews being black doesn't end there because history also gives us more undeniable proof.

It's defined as the study and practice of making maps and deals with the conception, production, and study of maps and charts. The modern form of this study, cartography, began to progress from the 6th Century BC onward. By the time we get to the Middle Ages, the maps that were produced used Jerusalem as the central feature and placed East at the top. Those representations are often called T-maps because they show only Europe, Asia, and Africa.

One such map is the 1766 Duke of Orleans map. On this particular map, there is an area in central West Africa called Lam-Lem. This area encompassed the country we know today as Nigeria. In the middle of this map, right below the word "Lam-Lem," it gives evidence of an area in that region that was apparently inhabited by Jews.

It says, "According to Edrifsi, the land hereabout was peopled by Jews." Edrifsi was actually Muhammad Al-Idrisi, a Muslim cartographer, geographer, traveler, and Egyptologist who was famous for his travels all over Europe, Africa, and Asia and mapping the regions he traveled in.

Al Idrisi is quoted as saying,

> "In the whole land of Lam-Lam (Nigeria-Cameroon-Chad-Niger) there are, but two small cities, or as it were villages, and those are Malel and Dau, situated at the distance of the four days journey from each other. Their inhabitants, as people of these parts relate, are JEWS, most of them unbelieving and ignorant."

So, according to Al Idrisi, the area we call Nigeria, Cameroon, Chad, and Niger was an area that was occupied by Jews.

This coincides with quotes from other sources that also mention Jews occupying West Africa before and after the slaves were brought to this country in 1619.

In the Memorandum for the President by Henry Kissinger, dated January 28, 1969, it says,

> "Biafra (3,000 sq. miles, 4-6 million). Colonel Ojukwu – 35, British-trained, erstwhile playboy – presides over the popular support, and military morale of a people convinced that defeat means extinction. The Ibos are the wandering Jews of West Africa -- gifted, aggressive, Westernized; at best envied and resented, but mostly despised by the mass of their neighbors in the Federation."

The Igbo people are one of the largest ethnic groups in Africa. They live mainly in southeastern Nigeria and speak Igbo, a language of the Benue-Congo branch of the Niger-Congo language family. What's interesting about the Igbo people is that there has been a lot of speculation about where the Igbo people came from. As of today, it is unknown how exactly the group came to form.

If Al Idrisi is correct, and there were Jews living in the Nigeria-Niger-Cameroon area, could it be that they migrated from Israel after the destruction of Jerusalem in 70 AD? Could it be that, because the persecution was coming from the north (Rome), they fled south into Africa and settled in West Africa? Could it be that the Igbos are, in fact, the Jews Al Idrisi says peopled the area called Lam-Lem? If the enemy is attacking from the North, would not the most logical route of escape be to go South? And since the Jews were living in Israel, going South could only lead them into Africa.

Have you ever wondered why African Americans in this country are called "Negroes?"

According to Oliver Thatcher in the book *Vasco da Gama: Round Africa to India*, the term "negro" is a term that was used by the Spanish and Portuguese when they arrived in Southern Africa around 1442. According to Stuart E Mann, in the book, "An Indo-European Comparative Dictionary," the term simply means black, and it was used to describe the Bantu peoples they encountered. Negro was also used of the peoples of West Africa in old maps labeled Negroland, an area stretching along the Niger River.

The Niger River is the principal river in West Africa. The river runs through the countries of Guinea, Mali, and Niger. It also runs along the border of the country of Benin before going through Nigeria. The main tributary for the Niger is the Benue River.

This is interesting because we just learned that the Igbo people live mainly in southeastern Nigeria, and their language is of the Benue-Congo branch of the Niger-Congo language family. The Niger runs right through the area the Igbos are known to occupy. This is also the same area Muhammad Al Idrisi said was occupied by Jews. This is the area the Portuguese called "Negroland." When you do a Google search, you'll find several of these "Negroland" maps.

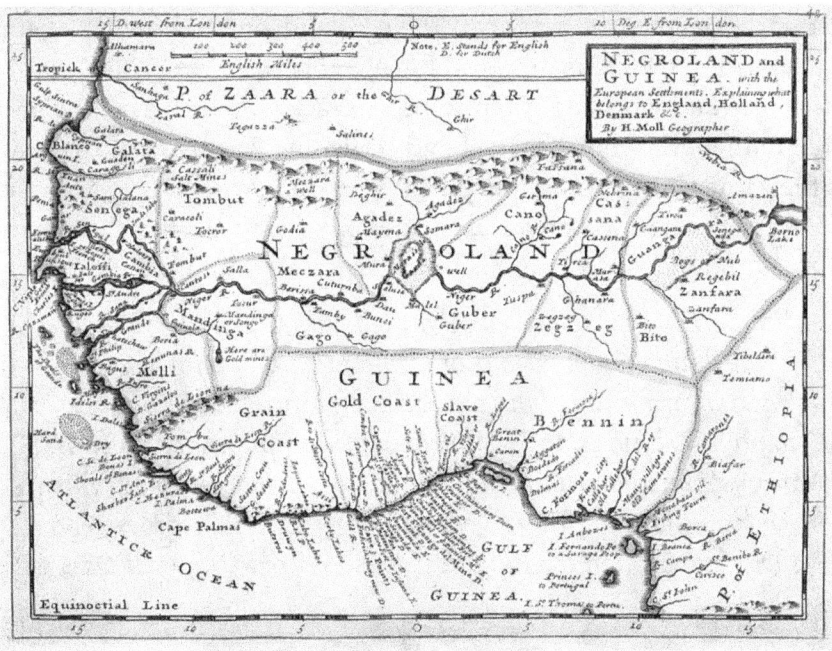

Image via: ("Negroland and Guinea with the European Settlements," Herman Moll, 1727, https://en.wikipedia.org/wiki/Guinea_(region)#/media/File:Negroland_and_Guinea_with_the_European_Settlements,_1736.jpg)

What's important to understand about these maps is that the entire continent of Africa was not called Negroland; it was only West Africa. That doesn't make much sense if the term "negro" meant black, and the people in Africa were all black. Why would they not name the entire continent Negroland?

It makes sense when you look at the Zondervan Compact Bible Dictionary. In referring to Noah's son Ham, it says,

> *"The youngest son of Noah, born probably about 96 years before the Flood; and one of eight persons to live through the Flood. He became the progenitor of the dark races; not the Negroes, but the Egyptians, Ethiopians, Libyans, and Canaanites."*

Ham was the progenitor (ancestor) of the dark races, not the Negroes? I thought all black people were Negroes? At least that's what we've been taught. But, according to Zondervan, only the Egyptians, Ethiopians, Libyans, and Canaanites are descendants of Ham. According to Zondervan, there is another group of black people on the earth who are not descendants of Ham. Those other black people were those who are defined as Negroes.

This means that the areas called Negroland, on all these 18th-century maps, were the areas occupied by Jews. So, the term "negro" was not just some random name given to us as black people. It was the name given to the Jews who left Israel and settled in West Africa. That's why it's the name given to black people in America.

George Fredrickson provides further proof of the difference between Negroes and other blacks in his book "The Black Mind," where he says,

> *"In the 1840s, Morton collaborated with George R. Gliddon, an Egyptologist, who provided him with mummy heads and information about the racial significance of Egyptian tomb inscriptions. In Crania Aegyptiaca, published in 1844, Morton pointed out that both cranial and archaeological evidence showed that Egyptians were not Negroes. The Negroes head was longer than the Egyptians heads (Fredrickson 2008)."*

Image via: ("British Map Kingdom of Judah West Africa," 1747, https://junglemaps.blogspot.com/2018/06/map-of-africa-that-says-judah.html

Image via: (Tribe of Judah, 1747, https://www.pinterest.com/pin/377669118733840648/

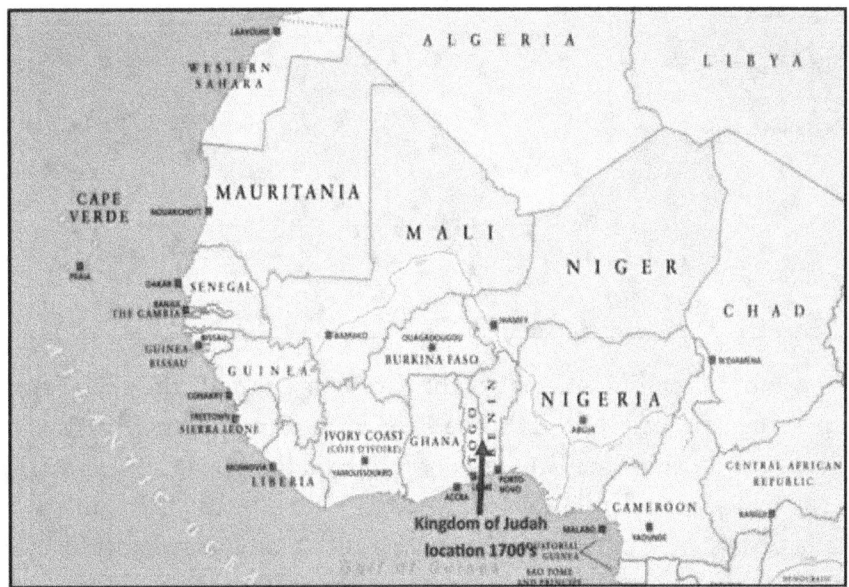

This is probably one of those moments where you just have to pause and say, "Wow." To learn that the reason why we're called Negroes in this country is because our ancestors were the original Hebrews has to be mind-blowing. It has to be one of those moments where you start to wonder how you could have missed this all these years. I know, for me, it felt as if someone had just uncovered the wool from over my eyes and brought me from darkness into light.

To add to that, when you look at a map of West Africa, you'll notice that the countries of Nigeria, Mali, Benin, and Niger are either on the coast or near the coast of West Africa. This is important, first of all, because this is the area in which the Jews migrated to after fleeing Israel. It is also the area in which many of the slaves were taken during the Transatlantic Slave Trade.

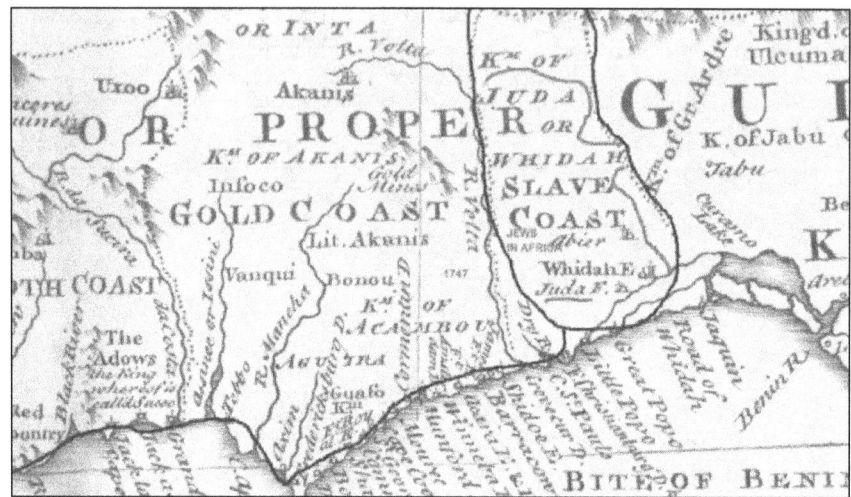

When you look at the 1747 map of the Kingdom of Judah, the 1720 British map of the Kingdom of Judah, the 1792 French map of the Kingdom of Judah, they all show the Kingdom of Judah on the West Coast of Africa.

The Kingdom of Juda (Whidah) can be seen in the area called the "Slave Coast," where the Portuguese first set up their slave port in 1580. On today's modern maps, this area is called Ouidah, which means Whydah or Judah. Today that area is known as the country of Benin. This is where the slaves were taken that would eventually be put on ships and transported to the Americas and other parts of the world.

It is believed that many of these slaves were Igbo. In describing the Igbo people, Wikipedia says:

> *"Chambers (2002) argued that many of the slaves taken from the Bight of Biafra across the Middle Passage would have been Igbo. These slaves were usually sold to Europeans by the Aro Confederacy, who kidnapped or bought slaves from Igbo villages in the hinterland. Igbo slaves may have not been victims of slave-raiding wars or expeditions, but perhaps debtors or Igbo people who committed within their communities alleged crimes. With the goal for freedom, enslaved Igbo people were known to the British colonists as being rebellious and having a high rate of suicide to escape slavery. There is evidence that traders sought Igbo women. Igbo women were paired with Coromantee (Akan) men to subdue the men because of the belief that the women were bound to their first-born sons' birthplace. It is alleged that European slave traders were fairly well informed about various African ethnicities, leading to slavers' targeting certain ethnic*

groups which plantation owners preferred. Particular desired ethnic groups consequently became fairly concentrated in certain parts of the Americas. The Igbo were dispersed to colonies such as Jamaica, Cuba, Saint-Domingue, Barbados, the future United States, Belize, and Trinidad and Tobago, among others (Holloway 2005)."

"Though thus separate from the African population, they are black and resemble the other Negroes in every respect as to physical character. It is probably in allusion to this case that Pennington, in his book, says, 'The descendants of a colony of Jews, originally from Judea, settled on the coast of Africa, are black (Wilson 1999).

Ulysses Santamaria describes the slave trade this way:

"Hundreds of thousands of slaves were transported to America from West Africa during the trade, which started some 400 years ago. What traces of Judaism still remained among the Negroes of West Africa at that period? To the extent that they were persecuted they were more than likely than other Negroes to be seized during wars and sold as slaves. It is virtually certain that many part Jewish Negroes were among those sent as slaves to America (Santamaria 1987)."

According to these writers, the slave traders were well informed of the various African ethnicities, and among these various Negro/Jewish people groups, the Igbo people were specifically targeted and seized to be taken as slaves.

That means that most, if not all, of the slaves that were brought to North America, South America, and the Caribbean were Igbos or of Hebrew descent. Even those who were "part Jewish Negroes" because of the intermarrying between Jews and other Africans (Egyptians, Ethiopians, Libyans, etc.), would have also been Jewish by blood. Could that mean that African Americans and those from Trinidad, Jamaica, Puerto Rico, Brazil, Colombia, Argentina, etc. are descendants of the Hebrews of West Africa? The answer is yes. There could be no other explanation.

If the Hebrews were the ones sold into slavery, there's no other explanation. All the evidence points to this one conclusion. The Hebrews, most likely the Igbos, fled Israel during the destruction of Jerusalem in 70 AD. After they fled, they settled in West Africa, in an area the Europeans would call Negroland. This area would be called Negroland because the people there would be different from the Egyptians, and Ethiopians, and Libyans, etc. Over time, because of cultural differences, and various other reasons, they would be sold into slavery by their neighbors.

I think that's a point of remembrance, that Africans played a direct role in the slave trade. Although it's not something we talk about a lot, it is still true nonetheless. Africans sold their captives, or prisoners of war, to European slave traders. Those who were sold were typically from neighboring or enemy ethnic groups. And, because the children of Israel didn't have the best of relationships with these neighboring nations, when the opportunity presented itself, those nations did what they could to rid the area of the despised Jews.

Israel's relationship with Egypt is a perfect example of how these other nations had no respect for the people of God. Remember, it was the Egyptians who enslaved the children of Israel for over 400 years. So, it's not a stretch to say that these Hebrews who fled into Africa, after fleeing Jerusalem, would eventually be sold into slavery by people who looked just like them.

The culture and the environment isn't like it is today where, if a black person sold another person into slavery, it would be against the law, and at the very least, looked down upon. At that time, selling blacks into slavery would not have been that big of a deal because both parties were black.

To be honest, after first learning all this, it didn't seem believable. Who would believe that we, as African Americans, are the descendants of the original Hebrews? It just doesn't seem real.

But then, when I read scripture, it validates this understanding even more.

In Jeremiah 17:4, it says,

> *"And you, even yourself shall let go of your heritage which I gave you; and I will cause you to serve your enemies in the land you do not know; for you have kindled a fire in My anger which shall burn forever."*

When you look at verse 1 in that same chapter, it tells us that He's talking to Judah. So, then the question is, "Have African Americans let go of their heritage? Have they served enemies in a land they do not know?" It is well known that, as African Americans, we don't know our heritage or where we came from. We can say we're from Africa, but that's about it. But Africa is a continent, so saying that we're from Africa doesn't tell us who we are or where we're from. In recent years, stay-at-home DNA testing has thrived. But for African Americans, genetic testing can create more questions and concerns than answers. Since people of European descent are the people who are widely tested, genetic biobanks have historically contained the DNA mostly of European people. As a result, there are scarce records for companies to pull from for people of color who sign up for testing("Lack of Diversity in Genetic Databases Hampers Research," Richard Harris, Aug.22, 2019, accessed September 14, 2020).

Although our people were a people of record-keeping, it was not in the way that would be accessible through the type of testing that is done today. We know that there was a lot of record keeping done through oral tradition. Unfortunately, a lot of that got lost over time, and now African Americans have let go of their heritage.

Have we served enemies in a land we do not know? The first slaves arrived in America in 1619. From 1619 to 1865, when the Thirteenth Amendment was passed, African Americans have been in a position of servitude in this country. We could even argue that African Americans are still in a position of servitude. So yes, we have served enemies in a land we do not know. That enemy can be defined as white America.

In Isaiah 11:12, it says,

> "He will set up a banner for the nations, and will assemble the outcasts of Israel, and gather together the dispersed of Judah from the four corners of the earth."

According to slavevoyages.org, between 1501 and 1866, over 12 million Africans were taken as slaves and dispersed all around the world. They would not only be brought to the United States, but they would also be taken to Denmark, France, the Netherlands, Great Britain, Spain, Brazil, Portugal, and Uruguay. Yet, God promises that one day, He will gather them from every corner of the Earth.

This promise is reiterated in Ezekiel 20:34, where He says,

> "I will bring you out from the people's and gather you out of the countries where you are scattered, with a mighty hand, with an outstretched arm, and with fury poured out."

I don't know about you, but when I read texts like this, only one group comes to mind. No other group of people has been scattered around the world the way black people have. The Europeans were not scattered. The Muslims weren't scattered. The Asians weren't scattered. The only people that were scattered were black people.

The most convincing proof that African Americans in this country are the original Hebrews is Deuteronomy 28. It's a chapter we often skim over because it lists these blessings and cursings that we've always thought applied to the children of Israel. For some reason, we've never really looked at the chapter in the context of the experiences of people of color in this country. Yet, when you go through the chapter, it's almost impossible to see this prophecy applying to anyone else.

Let's look at a few scriptures to see how the plight of African Americans in this country is eerily similar to those of the original Hebrews.

Deuteronomy 28:29-30 says,

> "And you shall grope at noonday, as a blind man gropes in darkness; you shall not prosper in your ways; you shall be only oppressed and plundered continually, and no one shall save you.
> You shall betroth a wife, but another man shall lie with her; you shall build a house, but you shall not dwell in it; you shall plant a vineyard, but shall not gather its grapes."

Sounds like slavery to me. "You shall be only oppressed and plundered. You shall betroth (marry) a wife, but another man shall lie with her. You shall build a house, but someone else will dwell in it." This is what our ancestors experienced during slavery.

Deuteronomy 28:32-33 says,

> "Your sons and daughters shall be given to another people, and your eyes shall look and fail with longing for them all day long; and there shall be no strength in your hand. A nation whom you have not known shall eat the fruits of your land and the produce of your labor, and you shall be only oppressed and crushed continually."

Deuteronomy 28:41 continues with,

> "You shall beget sons and daughters, but they shall not be yours; for they shall go into captivity."

During the slave trade, children were often unwilling participants who commonly found themselves enslaved as prisoners of warfare. In order for communities to make ends meet during times of famine, families would sometimes sell their children into slavery. There were also children who were used as pawns or bargaining chips to repay debts or crimes committed by their parents or relatives. Some parents even sold children who were in poor health, required special needs, or perceived as evil spirits. There were children who were purchased by slave owners and thus separated from their families. Then, of course, there were those, and are those who are currently being separated by mass incarceration and the child welfare system.

Deuteronomy 28:43 says,

> *"The alien (immigrant/foreigner) who is among you shall rise higher and higher above you, and you shall come down lower and lower."*

Did you know that the median White family has 10 times more wealth than the median Black family, but only 8 times more wealth than the median Latino family ("How U.S. Wealth Inequality Has Changed Since the Great Recession In Race, Ethnicity and Income," pewresearch.org, Nov.1,2017, accessed September 14, 2020).

Did you know that, when it comes to housing, 72 percent of White families own their own homes, compared to just 44 percent of Black families? Yet, 45 percent of all Latinos own their own homes. This is after a 40 percent increase between 1983 and 2016 (Pew Research Center, "Demographic Trends and Economic Well Being," June 27, 2016, accessed September 14, 2020).

Did you know that there are over 5 million white-owned businesses, almost 5 million Hispanic-owned businesses, but less than 3 million black-owned businesses in this country (Andrew Soergel, "Most of America's Businesses Run by White Men," Sept.1, 2016, accessed September 14, 2020)?

Did you know that, in most statistical categories, when it comes to wealth and upward mobility, immigrants consistently fare better than African Americans in this country?

We can also look at many of the liquor stores, and gas stations, and convenience stores, that populate black neighborhoods that are owned by everyone else but the residents themselves. Deuteronomy 28:46-48 says, *"And they shall be upon you for a sign and a wonder, and on your descendants forever. Because you did not serve the Lord your God with joy and gladness of heart, for the abundance of everything, therefore you shall serve your enemies, whom the Lord will send against you, in hunger, in thirst, in nakedness, and in need of everything; and He will put a yoke of iron on your neck until He has destroyed you."*

The curses of Deuteronomy 28 were to be a sign to African Americans, as well as to every other race, ethnicity, and nationality, that they were God's chosen people. No other group of people would experience what African Americans would experience in this country.

Deuteronomy 28:49 says,

> "The Lord will bring a nation against you from afar,
> from the end of the earth, as swift as the eagle flies,
> a nation whose language you will not understand."

This verse stands out in particular because it identifies the nation that would ultimately be responsible for the oppression that God's people would later experience. This would be a nation that is represented by an eagle (which is the national bird of the Unites States), which comes from afar (America is almost 9000 miles away from Africa), whose language they would not know (the original slave ship owners spoke languages that were unknown to the Africans who would later become slaves). All signs point to the United States of America.

Deuteronomy 28:61 says,

> "Also every sickness and every plague,
> which is not written in this Book of the Law,
> will the Lord bring upon you until you are destroyed."

Black Americans represent 13.4% of the American population, according to the US Census Bureau, but they account for more than half of all Covid-19 cases and more than half of all deaths due to the virus.

Since most black Americans have less than adequate healthcare and poorer living conditions, they tend to have more underlying health conditions, which makes them more likely to get sick and die from contracting the virus.

Black Americans have also been disproportionately affected by HIV/AIDS since the epidemic's beginning, and the disparity hasn't gotten better, it's only gotten worse.

Once again, even though they represent only 13% of the U.S. population, Blacks account for a much larger share of HIV diagnoses (43%), people estimated to be living with HIV disease (42%), and deaths among people with HIV (44%) than any other racial/ethnic group in the U.S. ("Black Americans and HIV/AIDS: The Basics," KFF. Org, Feb 07, 2020, accessed September 14, 2020).

No other race or ethnic group has been affected as much by sickness and disease as black people.

Deuteronomy 28:62 says,

> *"You shall be left few in number, whereas you were as the stars of heaven in multitude, because you would not obey the voice of the Lord your God."*

Even though there are no complete records as to how many slaves were taken from their homes during the slave trade, there are estimates that vary from a few million to 100,000,000 people. Most historians believe that between 9 and 11 million people were taken out of Africa by European slave traders and landed alive on the other side of the Atlantic.

We will never know the true total because there were enslaved people who died without ever reaching the Americas. There were also those who died at the hands of the African slave traders who took them from their homes in 'slave raids' in Africa. There were those who died on their way to the slave coast. Some died while waiting on the slave coast. Many died on the slave ships that took them across the Atlantic Ocean, from Africa to the Americas. Even though, at one time, they were as numerous as the stars of heaven, they would ultimately be left with few in number. Deuteronomy 28:64-67,

> *"Then the Lord will scatter you among all peoples, from one end of the earth to the other, and there you shall serve other gods, which neither you nor your fathers have known—wood and stone. And among those nations you shall find no rest, nor shall the sole of your foot have a resting place; but there the Lord will give you a trembling heart, failing eyes, and anguish of soul. Your life shall hang in doubt before you; you shall fear day and night, and have no assurance of life. In the morning you shall say, 'Oh, that it were evening!' And at evening you shall say, 'Oh, that it were morning!' because of the fear which terrifies your heart, and because of the sight which your eyes see."*

By the 1480s, Portuguese ships had begun taking African slaves from the continent of Africa. Their initial destinations were Cape Verde and the Madeira Islands in Portugal. By 1502 Spanish conquerors began taking slaves to the Caribbean. By the 1600s the Dutch had gotten involved. By the 1700s the English and French also began to export slaves.

Since there was not initially as much of a demand, there was only a few hundred thousand Africans taken before 1600. But, by the 17th century, due to the sugar plantations in the Caribbean and the tobacco plantations in America, demand increased. When demand increased, more Africans were taken and scattered around the globe.

In 1619 the first Africans arrived as slaves in Jamestown, a British colony of Virginia. For the next 246 years, they would be subjected to the worse treatment and conditions imaginable until the thirteenth amendment was ratified in December of 1865, abolishing slavery. After slavery was abolished, blacks had to deal with Jim Crow laws. These were laws meant to marginalize African Americans by denying them the right to get an education, hold a job, vote, as well as other opportunities. After the Jim Crow laws were eliminated in 1964 with the Civil Rights Act, blacks have had to deal with the KKK, mass incarceration, police brutality, racial profiling, stop and frisk, and the list goes on.

In every country where black people exist, we've had to deal with one thing or another. Most African Americans in this country can probably admit that at least one time in their life, they've felt as though their life was in doubt, or they were going to die, due to the color of their skin. As a result, black people have never been able to find rest or peace. Deuteronomy 28:68 says,

> "And the Lord will take you back to Egypt in ships,
> by the way of which I said to you, 'You shall never see it again.'
> And there you shall be offered for sale to your enemies
> as male and female slaves, but no one will buy you."

This might be the clearest and most obvious indicator in the entire chapter that points to African Americans in this country being the ancestors of the Hebrews of the Bible.

The text says that the Lord will take them back to Egypt in ships. The problem with that statement is that you can't take a ship to Egypt from Israel. When the Israelites traveled from Egypt to Israel, or vice versa, they went by foot. The reason they went by foot is because there is not a body of water that stretches from Egypt to Israel.

Even today, if you are traveling from Israel to Egypt, taking a boat is not an option. You can fly. You can walk. You can drive. But you can't take a boat. Even if there was a body of water, there wouldn't be enough boats big enough to take all of the Israelites back to Egypt. If a cruise ship carries about 2000 or more people, it would take a couple of hundred cruise ships to carry all the people to Egypt. And, we know that they wouldn't have had any boats that size anyway.

What's interesting is that the explanation of verse 68 is such a revealing topic that most commentaries won't even touch it. Out of the 20-30 commentaries I looked at to see how they explained it, there were literally only a few (3 or 4) that actually said anything about it. In those few, I saw explanations like, "the phrase is strange since people living in Canaan could travel to Egypt by land." There was another commentary that tried to explain it by saying that, by using the term "ships," the writer uses that word to say that "God would cause them to take a road on which they would never have been."

If you really take a minute and think about those explanations, none of them make any kind of sense. The Israelites never went back to Egypt in ships, and they never could. They could never go back to Egypt, physically in ships, if it were not even humanly possible. What we have to understand is that Egypt represents bondage. In Exodus 13:3 it says,

> "And Moses said to the people: 'Remember this day in which you went out of Egypt, out of the house of bondage; for by strength of hand the Lord brought you out of this place."

Exodus 20:2 says,
> "I am the Lord your God, who brought you out of the land of Egypt, out of the house of bondage."

Egypt is a metaphor for bondage. So when Moses says that the Lord would take His people back to Egypt in ships, what he's really saying is that they'll go back to bondage in ships- they will go back to being slaves by way of ships. That bondage happened when they were taken from Africa and sent to the Americas and the Caribbean as slaves.

Ask yourself, "Who else has gone through all of this?" The chances of all of these things happening to some other group of people are impossible.

So now, the question is why? Why have African Americans gone through all of this? The simple answer is disobedience.

In Deuteronomy 28:1-14, Moses lays out the blessings of obedience. In verses 15-68, he gives us the curses for disobedience. Because our ancestors were disobedient, we have had to experience all of these curses. I know that's not what we want to hear, but the reality is that it's true. How else can we explain why black people have had it so bad for all these years? No matter where we are or what we do, as a collective, we have had it enormously bad. The struggles that we have gone through and continue to go through cannot be explained in any other way.

And, I know some of you are thinking to yourself that that isn't fair. You're wondering why God would "punish" all of us for the sins of people that lived thousands of years ago. Well, it's the same reason we are "punished" for what Adam did thousands of years ago. Because of Adam's sin, all of us are born in sin and shaped in iniquity. Yet, if we accept Christ as Lord and Savior, we don't have to be under the penalty of sin. In the same way, if we as black people are obedient to Him, we will not suffer the curses the rest of our brethren experience.

So, now the question is, "Now that we know who the original Hebrews are, who are the people in Israel calling themselves Jews?"

We learned earlier that everybody is a descendant of one of Noah's three sons, Shem, Ham, and Japheth. Since the current occupants of Israel are white, it's obvious they can't be descendants of Shem or Ham because Shem and Ham were black. That means the people living in Israel now have to be from the line of Japheth. In other words, they must be European.

On the website science.mag.org, it says,

> "Modern Jews may traditionally trace their ancestry to the Holy Land, but a new genetic study finds otherwise. A detailed look at thousands of genomes finds that Ashkenazim – who make up roughly 80% of the world's Jews, including 90% of those in America and half of those in Israel – ultimately came not from the Middle East, but from Western Europe, perhaps Italy."

According to DNA, Ashkenazim, or Ashkenazi Jews, originated not in the Middle East, but Europe.

So, what is Ashkenazim, or an Ashkenazi Jew? When you go back to Genesis 10:3, you'll notice that Ashkenaz is a descendant of Japheth. Ashkenaz is the founder of Germany. Therefore, the Jews that occupy Israel at this moment are Jews whose ancestors originated in Germany. At some point, their ancestors converted to Judaism before moving to Israel. On the website *The Scientist*, it says,

> *"Most Ashkenazi Jews, traditionally believed to have descended from the ancient tribes of Israel, may, in fact, be maternally descended from prehistoric Europeans. The majority of Ashkenazi Jews are descended from prehistoric European women, according to a study published in Nature Communications. While the Jewish religion began in the Near East, and the Ashkenazi Jews were believed to have origins in the early indigenous tribes of this region, new evidence from mitochondrial DNA, which is passed on exclusively from mother to child, suggests that female ancestors of most modern Ashkenazi Jews converted to Judaism in the north Mediterranean around 2,000 years ago and later in west and central Europe."*

So, all these "Jews" we see on tv that are supposedly from Israel are not really from Israel. As we learned in the previous chapter where we talked about the lineage of the descendants of Japheth, their ancestors actually migrated from Germany to Israel after converting to Judaism. So, if we want to be real, they're really Gentiles living in Israel. What's crazy is, Jesus told us that Gentiles would inhabit Jerusalem. In Luke 21:24, He says, *"And they (Children of Israel) will fall by the edge of the sword, and be LED AWAY CAPTIVE into ALL nations. And JERUSALEM will be trampled by GENTILES until the times of the Gentiles are fulfilled."*

When slave ships came to Africa, the children of Israel were led captive into all nations. When it says that Jerusalem will be "trampled by the Gentiles," it means that Jerusalem would be taken over by the Gentiles until the "times of the Gentiles are fulfilled," or until the second coming of Jesus.

In Genesis 9:26-27, we find another example of the Bible prophesying beforehand that the Gentiles will occupy Jerusalem. Look at what it says,

> *"And he said: "Blessed be the Lord, The God of Shem, And may Canaan be his servant. May God enlarge Japheth, And may he dwell in the tents of Shem; And may Canaan be his servant."*

If you notice, the text says that Japheth would dwell in the tents or occupy the area that belongs to Shem. So, scripture is clear that the descendants of Japheth (Gentiles) would inhabit Jerusalem.

So how did these Gentile Jews take over Jerusalem if that isn't really their home? That's a good question. If you remember, in 70AD, when Jerusalem was destroyed, all the original Hebrews fled South. After they fled, the city was desolate. Eventually, the Gentile Jews moved in and occupied the land. That's why they currently occupy the home that was originally given to God's chosen people.

Did you know that, according to the Melanoma Foundation, at one time, Israel had one of the highest rates of melanoma, the deadliest form of skin cancer? Melanoma is caused by too much exposure to the sun's ultraviolet rays. Did you know that Jews consistently have high rates of melanoma? Did you know that the reason they have such a high rate is because they are in an area of the world that is not conducive to their body type (Richard David Kahn, "Why Israel's Skin Cancer Rates Are Dropping," last modified July 19, 2019, accessed September 14, 2020)?

God never created them to live in that part of the world (Remember Israel is actually North Africa). Because of a lack of melanin, they are more susceptible to getting cancer when they are outside in the sun for prolonged periods of time. That's why it makes no sense to believe that the original Hebrews were white when it would have been impossible for them to survive the Egyptian heat. The only reason they can survive in Israel (which is still North Africa) is because they have learned to get out of the sun. There was also this invention called sunscreen, which helps them from being burned by the sun as much.

What about the Jewish names? If they aren't Jewish, how did they get names like Epstein, and Goldberg, and Horowitz, etc.?

In 1787 there was a law called the Austro-Hungarian Law that essentially required the Jews living in Germany to register a permanent family surname. It was also required that this name be German. The law required that all surnames that were used previously in reference to Jewish families be abandoned. The names that were chosen were then subject to approval. If a name was not chosen, one was assigned.

This means that all of those names ending in -berg (Goldberg), and stein (Einstein), and witz (Horowitz), and feld (Seinfeld, Berkenfeld), and blum (Rosenblum) are all German names. They have absolutely nothing to do with whether a person is a Jew or not.

Arab Nation

Anytime we talk about black people being the original occupants of North Africa, one of the topics that always seems to come up is this belief that, when we look at the Middle East today, and even in Egypt and other northern African countries, the people there are not black but Arab, or lighter in complexion. That leads many to dispel the notion that the Middle East was, at one time, all black and considered a part of North Africa. It also feeds into the false belief that Israel was not originally filled with black people.

What many don't understand is that the only reason the people in the Middle East are lighter in complexion today is because of the Muslim Conquests in the 7th century when the Muslims invaded North Africa, and because of the mixing of Africans with non-blacks. Before that, all of Africa, including the Middle East, was black.

In the *Encyclopedia of the Jewish Diaspora*, it says,

"The decline of the Jewish communities of the West Africa-Maghreb most likely began with the influx of Arab invaders into North Africa starting in 640 CE and later into West Africa in the 1300s and 1400 CE (M. Avrum Ehrlich 2008).

In *Babylon to Timbuktu*, it's even clearer when the author says,

"There was an Indo-European invasion (Germanic) of the Middle East between the years 2000 and 1500 B.C. These Germanic tribes intermingled with the black people everywhere they traveled. This mingling made the people in Syria, Babylon, Assyria, Persia, India, and parts of the Arabia much lighter in complexion. Now, the color of the people in this region ranges from brown to yellow. The Greek and Roman invasions also made these people in the Middle East lighter. Another fact we should not forget is that the Moors and Arabs from North Africa captured and raped European women. As a result, the North Africans became lighter. At one time, these people in North Africa and the Middle East were all black (Windsor 23)."

Therefore, the original inhabitants of North Africa were black. They only became "lighter" after the conquests and the intermingling of black people with non-blacks.

Black Jesus

One of the biggest elephants in the room that needs to be addressed is the question of whether or not Jesus was black. That's a question that, to be honest, most people don't want to discuss. A lot of people like to say that it doesn't matter what color Jesus was. But, I think that's their way of not wanting to make people uncomfortable, because we've all been conditioned to believe Jesus was white. What I do think is interesting is that everybody seems to think it doesn't matter what color Jesus is when somebody starts talking about Him not being white. You even have people of color subscribing to this. But, I think it does matter what color Jesus was. It matters because, if He was black (which He was), that means there's been an intentional coverup for almost the last 2000 years.

Just think of what it would mean if it came out that Jesus was black. It would change the view of Christianity as we know it. For one, we'd get to see who the real racists are because no racist will follow a black Jesus. No racist would acknowledge that a black man is God. I can imagine that would really mess some white folks up. All this time, they've been thinking that they've been serving a white Jesus, but now they find out that Jesus is black, it would change everything.

If it came out that Jesus was black, I think it would also change how people of color view Jesus. It would also change how they view Christianity as a whole. Whereas some believe it's a white man's religion, many would begin to come back to Christianity or come to Christianity for the first time.

So what color was Jesus?

To answer that question, let's go back two thousand years ago to a city called Jerusalem. King Herod has issued a decree that all newborn Hebrew baby boys be killed. Joseph, Jesus' father, has a dream where an angel warns him to take Jesus and his mother into Egypt (Matthew 2:13, NKJV). The purpose of going to Egypt is to hide Jesus and to prevent Him from being killed. If Jesus were white like He is always portrayed in movies and pictures, how would He be able to blend in among all the black Egyptians in Egypt? It would be impossible for Him not to stand out if He was white. Remember, Egyptians didn't begin to have lighter skin until the Muslim Conquests.

In Matthew 1, we find the lineage of Jesus. In that lineage, we find that it begins with Abraham. We already learned that Abraham was black, which would mean that everybody after him would be black. But, even so, in that same lineage, we find Jacob and Judah, whom we learned were both black as well. We also know that Jesus was from the tribe of Judah. We learned previously that the line of Judah was black. And, although we understand that Jesus' "biological" father wasn't Joseph, we know that Joseph was black because he was also from the line of Judah.

Therefore, when Jesus was born and is said to be from the line of Judah, would He not look like His earthly parents and the tribe in which they descended from? In other words, why would the Bible clearly mention that Jesus was from the tribe of Judah if He didn't look like the people from that tribe?

We find more proof when we look at scriptures where His appearance is actually described. A perfect example is in Daniel 10:5-6, where Daniel sees a Being that can only be described as Christ. We know that because we find a similar description in Revelation 1. In Daniel 10:4-6, it says,

> "Now on the twenty-fourth day of the first month, as I was by the side of the great river, that is, the Tigris, I lifted my eyes and looked, and behold, a certain man clothed in linen, whose waist was girded with gold of Uphaz! His body was like beryl, his face like the appearance of lightning, his eyes like torches of fire, his arms and feet like burnished bronze in color, and the sound of his words like the voice of a multitude."

In Revelations 1:12-15, it says,

> "Then I turned to see the voice that spoke with me. And having turned I saw seven golden lampstands, and in the midst of the seven lampstands One like the Son of Man, clothed with a garment down to the feet and girded about the chest with a golden band. His head and hair were white like wool, as white as snow, and His eyes like a flame of fire; His feet were like fine brass, as if refined in a furnace..."

What color is burnished bronze? Burnished bronze is dark brown. This is the color Daniel sees when he looks at this Being's arms and feet. When John sees Him, he sees feet that are brass, which is the same color as burnished bronze. He also sees hair that is white like wool, as white as snow. We know that wool isn't straight. In fact, wool is rather kinky. So, the person that Daniel and John see has arms and feet that are dark brown, and hair that is kinky. Those features sound very similar to that of a black man.

In Genesis 1:26, the Bible says that God made man in His image. In Genesis 2:7, it says that man (God's image) was made from the dust (dirt) of the ground. Everybody knows that dirt is brown. Actually, dirt is dark brown. So if God made man in His image, and man was made from dark brown dirt, that could only mean that, when God became flesh and came to this earth, His complexion was that of a black man.

Can you see the irony in that? With everything that is taking place in this country, in regards to the treatment of black people, isn't is ironic that, when the Savior of the world came to this earth, He came as a black man? I wonder if, or how, things might change if the world knew that the identity of Jesus was stolen and made to fit the identity of Europeans.

CHAPTER 7

Black People and the Sabbath

Whenever you read books or hear people talk about the presence of black people in scripture, for some reason, you never hear anybody address the importance of the Sabbath. Some may wonder, "What does the Sabbath have to do with the presence of black people in scripture?"

Well, to be honest, it's almost impossible to talk about African Americans as the ancestors of the original Hebrews without talking about the Sabbath. It's impossible because the Sabbath was foundational to the life of a Jew. During the time of Christ, it was part of the commandments God gave to Moses on Mt. Sinai. In addition to that, most Christians today associate the Sabbath with the Jews (even though it wasn't just for the Jews). So, how can you really have a conversation about how black people need to know who they are without also calling them back to keeping God's Holy Sabbath day?

I can imagine, for most of us, we were probably taught at an early age that Sunday was the day of worship. The justification for this particular teaching was that Jesus rose from the dead on Sunday, and since Jesus rose on Sunday, Sunday is the new day of worship- better yet, Sunday is the Christian Sabbath. The problem is that the Bible doesn't teach that the Sabbath was changed from Saturday to Sunday. That means that Sunday was never a day of worship.

In scripture, God's people always kept the seventh-day Sabbath. The reason is because the Sabbath, not Sunday, was given at creation (Genesis 2:1-3, NKJV). Jesus and His disciples kept the Sabbath (Luke 4:16; Luke 13:10, NKJV). Even after Jesus died, the disciples continued to keep the

Sabbath on the seventh day (Luke 23:54-24:1; Acts 13:14,42,44; Acts 18:4, NKJV). It wasn't until the Roman Emperor Constantine made a decree, mandating Sunday worship, that people began to worship God on the first day of the week. Before that, all Christians worshiped on the seventh-day Sabbath. This is validated by scripture as well as history. If you Google, "Who changed the Sabbath," you'll learn that it was the Roman Catholic Church that instituted the change.

Since the early Christians were initially Jewish, they obviously were sabbath-keepers. When they became Christians, they continued to keep the Sabbath because the Sabbath was given to all people at creation, over 1500 years before the Jews existed. When the Jews eventually became Christian, they continued keeping it because they knew God had given it to Adam and Eve the day after they were created.

Although many would stop keeping the Sabbath, because of Constantine's decree, the Sabbath has always been kept in Africa. The Sabbath is so ingrained in the life of the African people that, in Ghana, Saturday (Sabbath) is called "Onyamee Kwame's" day. The reason they call it this, is because according to the Akan tradition (an African tribe that inhabits southern Ghana and the Ivory Coast), when a child is born, he's given a name depending on which day of the week it is.

So, if he's born on Monday, he's given the name Kwadwo. If he's born on Tuesday, it's Kwabena. If he's born on Saturday, it's Kwame. If it's Sunday, it's Kwasi, and so on. There are also different names for females born on different days. But since God rested on Saturday (Sabbath), He's called Onyamee, or Onyankopon Kwame- meaning the God of Saturday. Therefore, the African people have always recognized the Sabbath as God's day.

The Sabbath is such an integral part of the Akan tradition that they recognize the outside influences that attempted to change it. For instance, in the Akan tradition, the white man is called "broni," or "obroni." And, because they recognize that it was the white man that brought Sunday worship to Africa, white people are sometimes called "kwasi broni," which means Sunday white man.

So, the people of West Africa recognize that Sunday was never God's day. They recognize that Sunday was the day the pagans used to worship the sun-god. They know that it wasn't until the white man came to Africa, and brought his Europeanized version of Christianity, that black people began to worship on the first day of the week. If the white missionaries never came to Africa bringing their form of Christianity, black people today would be keeping God's seventh-day Sabbath. This is why it's so important that we, as black people, understand why we do what we do. If we did, we would all be following the example of Jesus by keeping the Sabbath day holy.

In his book *The Akan Saturday God of Saturday*, an Ashanti Ghanian named Kofi Owusu-Mensa says,

> *"The Akan peoples of Ghana worshiped the Creator on Saturday long before the first Portuguese ship anchored off the coast in 1471. Ashante records have it that in the 1920s, the queen mother and women of Ashante presented a silver stool as a gift to Princess Mary of Britain, through the British governor, and in an accompanying message, the queen mother alluded to the Akan God of Saturday, Onyamee Kwame."*

> *The queen mother said, "We pray the great God Nyankopon, on whom men lean and do not fall, whose day of worship is a Saturday, and whom the Ashanti serve just as Princess Mary serves Him, that He may give the king's child and her husband long life and happiness, and finally, when she sits upon this silver stool, which the women of Ashanti have made for their White queen mother, may she call us to mind."*

So, the Sabbath has always been a part of Africa- it's just that the rest of humanity has been late to the party.

In Exodus 20, there's the story of God giving Moses the Ten Commandments on Mt. Sinai. In verse 2, God begins the Decalogue by saying, *"I am the Lord your God, who brought you out of the land of Egypt, out of the house of bondage."* He then goes on to give Moses the Ten Commandments. God begins by referencing Egypt because He wanted to remind them of where they came from – that they used to be slaves. And, because they were no longer slaves, they were to keep His commandments- one of which was to "Remember the Sabbath day, to keep it holy."

In Deuteronomy, God does the same thing. In Deuteronomy 5, the commandments are restated. In verses 12-14, He repeats the Sabbath command. But then, in verse 15, He says, "And remember that you were a slave in the land of Egypt, and the Lord your God brought you out from there by a mighty hand and by an outstretched arm; therefore the Lord your God commanded you to keep the Sabbath day."

So once again, God is keeping before them the fact that they were once slaves. Since they were once slaves and have now been set free, they ought to keep the Sabbath. As the ancestors of God's chosen people, who were also once slaves, because we are now free, we also ought to keep the Sabbath.

CHAPTER 8

Who Cares?

Jesus was black. Moses was black. Abraham was black. The children of Israel were black. African Americans are the true Hebrews. The Garden of Eden was in Africa. The Gentiles aren't all non-Jews. So what? I can imagine that may be the response of some. Who cares whether or not most of the bible characters were black? Since God doesn't care about color, why should we?

We shouldn't care about color, but we should definitely care about whether or not the Bible characters we've been led to believe were white, were really black. The reason we should care is because it proves, once again, to what extent some Europeans will go to promote their agenda of white supremacy. Whatever they have to do to suppress people of color, that's what they will do, even if it means painting Jesus, and everybody else, white.

So, it's not simply about a color. It's about refusing to accept the lie that some people in this country and around the world continue to perpetuate at the expense of people of color.

For years our story has always been told as if it began in 1619. But, when we read scripture, it is evident that not only did black people exist before we arrived in this country as slaves, but in Africa, we thrived. So to allow anyone to continue to tell the story that important biblical figures were only white, and for us to continue to accept it as fact, would be a detriment to us as a people. Our history has its beginning in Genesis, and we shouldn't accept any other account.

We should also care about what we've learned because it proves that, as African Americans, not only do we have a place in Christianity, but it was the black man that started Christianity. Therefore Christianity is not the white man's religion; it's the black man's religion, too.

In 2008 something happened that was the first in this country's history- a black man, Barack Obama, became President of the United States of America. It was a moment black Americans thought they'd never see. When he became president, African Americans were excited, not just because a black man was now the most powerful person in the world, but also because black boys and girls had someone they could strive to be. They now had representation in the highest office of the land. The 13-year-old black boy from Washington D.C. and the 8-year-old black girl from the Bronx now had proof that anything was possible. If a black man named Barack Obama could make it, they could also make it as well.

But imagine that same black boy, or that same black girl finding out that the Savior of the world looked just like them. Imagine what kind of confidence that would instill, not just in them, but in all of black America.

One of the problems with continuing to see God in an image that looks nothing like yourself is that it creates the belief that the image represented is superior, and you are inferior. Once that becomes ingrained in your mind, you begin to believe that you aren't as worthy as everyone else. Your actions then begin to follow your mind.

How that relates to the importance of learning that the Bible is black history is that, if you have internalized the view that Jesus has a nationality and physical characteristics different from yourself, then you automatically assume that you are inferior in your own characteristics. When you have this sense of inferiority you begin to believe you have less potential than the individual who looks like the image. This is why it's so important to know that Jesus was a black Man, and that the Bible is black history.

References

Akbar Ph.D, Na'im, "Breaking the Chains of Psychological Slavery," Mind Productions and Associates Inc, 1996

Armstead, Wilson, "A Tribute for the Negro: Being a Vindication of the Moral, Intellectual, and Religious Capabilities of the Colored Portion of Mankind; with Particular Reference to the African Race," Electronic Edition; 1848

Barnes, Jonathan, "Complete Works of Aristotle, Vol.2: The Revised Oxford Translation Volume 193 of Bollingen Series (General) Series, 1984

Dalton Jr, Ronald, "Hebrews to Negroes: Wake Up Black America," G Publishing, LLC, 2014

Fredrickson, George M., "The Black Image in the White Mind: The Debate on Afro-American Character and Destiny, 1817–1914," Wesleyan University Press, 1987

Manilius. Astronomica. Edited and translated by G. P. Goold. Loeb Classical Library 469. Cambridge, MA: Harvard University Press, 1977.

McKissic, William Dwight, "Beyond Roots: In Search of Blacks in the Bible," Renaissance Productions, 1990

Warden Jr, James H., "Blacks in the Bible: The Original Roots of Men and Women of Color in Scripture," *Have You Heard the Good News*, 2015

Windsor, Rudolph R, "From Babylon to Timbuktu: A History of Ancient Black Races Including The Black Hebrews," *Windsor Golden Series*, 1969

About The Author

Keenan West is a pastor who was born in Wilmington, DE, but raised in Washington, D.C. He holds a Bachelors in Theology with a minor in Biblical Languages. He also has a Masters in Pastoral Studies. He has a passion for preaching the Gospel, and loves seeing people come out of darkness into His marvelous light. Keenan has a heart for the community and enjoys following Christ's example of ministering to those in need. He is married to Dr. Jeneen West and has three beautiful children, Kaia, Kelsi, and Kohen.